The Dance
of the Lion
and the Unicorn

The Secret of
Conscious Relationships

Mark Waller, Ph.D

WingSpan Press

Printed in the United States of America

Parts of this book are a work of fiction. Names, characters, settings and incidents are either the product of the author's imagination or used fictitiously. Any resemblance to actual events, settings or persons, living or dead, is entirely coincidental.

Cover photograph by Mark Waller

Published by WingSpan Press, Livermore, CA
www.wingspanpress.com

The WingSpan name, logo and colophon are the trademarks of WingSpan Publishing.

ISBN 1-978-59594-128-2

First edition 2007

Library of Congress Control Number 2006939630

Acknowledgments

People who come to a psychotherapist's office are more often than not dealing with a lot of unacknowledged pain. It is my privilege and honor to see into their hearts into the crucible of the pain and defenses that have been constructed to deal with that pain.

This experience has been my teacher. So I would be remise in not acknowledging those who come to me for help for they are my greatest assets in my own growth and insight into the human condition, mine as well as theirs.

I would like also to acknowledge my agent, Paul Cash. His belief in this project has been a source of enormous encouragement. His editing skills have made a monumental contribution to the readability and clarity of the prose.

Of special note is Reverend Kristina Collins. She has been a friend of mine and a friend of this work. Also, Reverend Annette Drake for giving my work the boost it need one hot July evening. Thank you to Alan Cohen who wasn't too busy to actually read and endorse my work. What a blessing! I want to thank Joann Turner, my editor at The Messenger who believes in Lion and Unicorns and lets me write a column about it.

Dr. Richard Young has been a good friend. Every time he thought he could help, he did in an unselfish manner. His generosity and friendship is much appreciated. There are many early readers of the work that gave me valuable feedback and encouragement. Most of those I cannot mention due to confidentiality. And to any I may have forgotten, I sincerely apologize.

Epigraph

No problem can be solved from the same consciousness that created it.

- Albert Einstein

Contents

Illustrations

Contents

Preface

I am a marriage and family therapist sitting with Matt and Jeanie, who have come to see me after being married for eight years. In this first stage of therapy, they're using my time and their money to fight and squabble. I listen to them blame one another. Neither one wants to take any responsibility for contributing to the problems in their relationship. Every now and then, I have to calm them down. Since we have a rapport built up over a few sessions, they are no longer embarrassed by their behavior in front of me. Such is the value of rapport. I watch them carefully, looking for an opening to shift their attention from their fight to more productive work. Suddenly, like a clear blue light shining in the back of my head, I see a pattern. It's a pattern I have seen over and over again. But this time it takes on an unexpected animation.

When I first saw this pattern, I thought that it could be explained by what happened in those early critical years of learning, while the brain of the still-fragile child is rapidly growing. I had looked at it through the lens of childhood development, and I had seen at least part of the answer. Now I'm seeing deeper, into the heart of the beast.

While Matt listens to his wife rage at him, he gets a remote look in his eyes. Suddenly he shows a kind of deer-in-the-headlights "look"; his nose becomes more of a snout and a large, twisted thing starts growing out of his forehead. I stare in disbelief. My God! What's happening here? Before I know it, he has transformed into a large horse with the tail of a lion and a dangerous horn.

Jeanie does not notice this, but her rants sound like a throaty growl. Her long brown hair begins to change. She bares her teeth and roars. She rears back on her haunches and begins to lick her forearm.

They've turned into a Unicorn and a Lion right before my eyes. I've seen this transformation before, but have never been so aware of it. Many couples have shown this Lion and Unicorn pairing, but it has never before appeared so obvious. Thinking back, I can remember seeing the shadow of a Lion or the silhouette of a Unicorn very near a person. But like so many of life's apparitions, I had brushed these visions aside. A therapist is a trained observer of people. Possibly, I could be forgiven for never having noticed the beasts within.

My concentration drifts back to Matt and Jeanie. The transformation is now complete. Jeanie is pacing. She tosses her mane wildly. Her claws scratch the ground as she tries to pick up his scent with a powerful sniff of her moist, black nose. Her head slunk down between her shoulders, she lurks through the tall grass of the Serengeti. Every now and then, she raises her head and sniffs the breeze.

Far across the plain, Matt is climbing Kilimanjaro looking for safe haven. At the first sign of her growl, he bolted. His powerful haunches launching him beyond her reach, he seems almost to disappear into thin air.

I recall there was an instant of snorting and a whinny from his lungs. There was the telltale sound of hooves clicking on the tile floor in the waiting room just before he galloped off. Powerful strides moved him well beyond her. Am I only imagining that I saw the scars of claw marks on his back?

Their arguing has reached a crescendo and neither seems to have the heart for the fight anymore. She sits in the chair, exhausted from the hunt. I can only imagine the frustration she feels after the effort of the pursuit that ended in failure. Noticing her spent condition, he reappears. His nostrils expand as he gasps to catch his breath.

I look at them and gather my senses, knowing what I have seen: She is a Lion and he is a Unicorn. They can no longer hide their reality from me. I wonder how much longer they can hide it from themselves. I can tell from the looks of guilt and surprise in their eyes that they know some sort of transformation took place. They know that in some fashion they were not themselves. But I'm aware that they didn't see it. It was as if they themselves had been pushed aside. The two adults were co-opted by two beasts lurking inside that were determined to get out and take control.

How is this transformation like those I have seen before? I scan my memory for other couples. The Lions weren't always women. Sometimes the man was the more ferocious of the two. And just as often a woman would turn into a Unicorn. So gender is not a rule for how the transformation will occur.

But one thing does seem a stable part of the pattern. I think back over the hundreds of couples who have been in my office, and realize that nearly every one has been comprised of a Lion and a Unicorn. Dear Lord! What can it mean? Why does every relationship seem to have this predator and prey—pursuer/pursued setup?

Only later, after dozens of more experiences with different couples am I able to study this bestial transformation more closely. I ultimately have to remove the glasses through which I could see only the effects of childhood development. I know, of course, that those first critical years can't be ignored; so I clean those glasses carefully to remove any distortion. What I saw was so obvious that I wondered why it had never before occurred to me.

I am looking at temperament! Of course, temperament. Why not temperament? How could I have been so blind? The Lion and the Unicorn have been there all along. But it was like one of those puzzles in those children's magazines I used to see in the dentist's office. There was a big picture of a jungle and the caption said, "There are a Lion and a Unicorn in the jungle, see if you can find them."

That's why I never saw them before. I kept looking at the "forest" of childhood development without seeing the "trees" of temperament that had been planted there before birth. But when I lay the template of psychology over temperament, I finally get the big picture.

Each person can be seen as sitting on a three-legged stool: one leg for temperament, one leg for neurological development, and one leg for attachment and social learning. Relationships can be seen as the basic interplay of the Unicorn and the Lion. The way people organize their behavior comes from early brain development. The intensity of the problems in the relationship is a direct result of the quality of attachment and social learning that developed in those formative years.

Now I see relationship as a dance—an interplay—as opposed to armed conflict. For the day I saw the Lion and the Unicorn emerge, I saw the dance between them. At the same time, I was able to understand the secret language of relationships.

Mark Waller
Chino Hills, CA
November 2004

Chapter 1

The First Phone Call

"You do marriage counseling?" asks the voice on the other end of the phone. There is irritation, an edge in her voice.

"Yes, that's mainly what I do."

"Well, we need it. Do we both need to come? He says he will if you want him to be there."

"Actually, that would be preferable," I answer, thinking back on the difference having both parties in the room makes. Most therapists would rather not do couples' therapy. It's hard work, and the experience can be unnerving. There's normally a lot of conflict and emotion in the room, and a fine line between being a leader and a referee.

"When can we come and see you? We need to come right away."

I bring my calendar up on the screen and check my schedule. "Would tomorrow night at 7:00 work for you? I had a cancellation this morning and that time became available."

"That will be fine."

I give her directions to my office and repeat my number even though I know she just called it. "Please give me a call and confirm you're coming. I've reserved the time exclusively for you."

"Don't worry. We'll be there!" she says, and I hear the receiver clatter in its cradle just before the line goes dead.

I hope they will come. So often, strangely enough, just calling and asking for help relieves enough pressure that the potential client feels better and doesn't bother to show up for the first appointment.

I make a few more entries in my calendar, saying a silent prayer as I do. It may sound funny that I pray; but I've found from experience that helping people often involves something greater than myself. This realization has made me a spiritual person, though not a conventionally religious one.

Couples most often come to a counselor on their way to a lawyer. This can put me in a tough spot if I let it. I say, "If I let it," because often one of the partners will try to make saving the marriage *my* responsibility. Buying in to that agenda can be more dangerous to me than to them. If I fail to "save the marriage," I'll have many a bad day after the whole thing blows up.

More often than not, problems in a relationship have been brewing for years. It's not fair to me if the entire burden of this falls on my shoulders. But I'm human, and so are my clients, and sometimes people pay a heavy price for freedom and fulfillment. We often put ourselves through enormous pain in the process of awakening to our true nature and discovering our secret emotional needs.

The Moment Arrives

I'm finishing up with Art as I hear the door to my office open and the muffled voices of Pat and Angie entering the waiting room. Art has been talking almost continuously for 50 minutes about his girlfriend. Every two or three weeks they get into an argument over something that he feels is inconsequential and she feels is of biblical proportions. She rages at him (his version). He acts calm and reasonable and tries to explain himself, which makes her even more distraught. She breaks off the relationship, and he ignores her until she calls. They make up, make love, and make plans for the future. Then the cycle starts again.

"We ordered these flowery drapes for when she moves in with me. Now what the hell am I supposed to do with these goddamn drapes? I don't want any flowers on drapes. Next thing you know I'll be putting flamingo statues in the front yard!"

"You seem really upset, Art. This relationship seems to put a real strain on you."

"Strain on me? Hell, I'm not strained. *She's* strained."

This has been the tenor of the conversation for the hour. This has been the tenor of the conversation every session for six months. Mercifully, the hour is almost up.

"Gosh," I say, "this seems oddly like the exact same story you told me three weeks ago—about the party you went to where she got jealous?"

Art laughs, "I guess it does."

"I wonder if there's anything to look at in these patterns, Art?"

"I think she just needs to calm down. That's the problem!"

I take a deep breath and hope blood doesn't start spurting from my tongue. Of course, there's a pattern at work. I saw it during our first session. I've told him the pattern. I've diagrammed it on the whiteboard next to my chair. I've explained, in detail, where it comes from.

He nods, he acknowledges what I say, and acts like a person engaged in a meaningful conversation; but he doesn't really hear a word I say.

Art is a Unicorn raised by an intrusive and emotionally needy mother. His early interactions with his mother established a defensive structure within him that constantly creates distance while hiding an enormous need for acceptance. I find myself wondering if his defenses will ever open even a crack. God knows I've tried everything short of a craniotomy to penetrate the emotional lobotomy he got in the relational space with his mother. It is hard to sit here with an insight that could change his life drastically for the better, and watch him squirm and consistently, persistently, not get it.

As Art exits, I motion Pat and Angie into my office. They seem to be in their mid 30s. Pat has a relatively light grip on my hand as we shake. Angie is short and I would guess about 30 pounds overweight, but attractive. She has a full head of jet-black hair, a beautiful face, and some Latin blood that gives her a slightly exotic look.

They look tense as I explain my background, qualifications, and experience. "Before we get started," I ask, "do you have any questions about me, or the counseling process?"

They shrug their shoulders, and I hand them my "informed consent form." I explain that they're acknowledging that I'm a "mandated reporter," which means that I have to report child abuse and elder abuse. It talks about confidentiality and spells out that I'm their therapist and not their friend. This means that as their therapist I will masquerade as a friend, do the things a friend would do, and say the things a friend would say—until they walk out my office door. But if I run into them on the street, I can't wave and say hello. I can't acknowledge them unless they acknowledge me first. In general, I will act as if I am not a friend. So they must learn to like and respect me even though I'm a stranger who acts like a friend.

Furthermore, there will be consequences of them not treating me like a friend. If they don't pay me promptly there will be consequences. If they don't show for an appointment or give me 24 hours' notice, I will do unfriendly things. They must understand that, unlike friends, we have to honor therapeutic boundaries. Violate these boundaries and our pseudo-friendship becomes something different.

Much of what I tell them comes dictated from the State, which feels it knows considerably more about friendship than I do, since I have no friends and they have so many. In short, I must be a professional who cares, and not a friend.

This has some benefits to the client as well. For instance, their therapist doesn't approach them in a restaurant and ask in a loud voice, "So, how's the alcohol problem?" or "Are you still beating your wife?"

Still there is no substitute for emotional maturity, judgment, personal growth, and awareness in a counselor. The State can't ensure that exists in a candidate, although they do try hard, in the licensing process, to use the process to get the best candidates they can.

I can tell that Pat and Angie want me to get to the point, so I ask: "Well, what brings you here?"

Simultaneously they point to one another and say, "He/She does!" They have learned the first and most fundamental rule of a dysfunctional relationship: blame. Blame tells you that everything you don't like is a function of the other person. This is a fortunate point of view, as it alleviates having to take responsibility for your own emotional reactions. Taking responsibility takes considerably more effort than blaming, so blaming is far more convenient and handy.

"He never talks to me. He doesn't listen. He doesn't care!"

"That's not true," he protests. "It's just that I believe people can work things out by remaining calm. God, Angie, you are never calm." He turns to me with a desperate look in his eye and says, "Look, Doc, you're my last hope. I just can't put up with the constant arguments, the fighting. I've started to look for an apartment. I've got to get away from this. I can't take it any more."

With that, Angie starts to cry hard into a tissue. "I don't know what I will do if he leaves me. He is the love of my life." She looks at me. "What do I do?"

I can tell that his calmness is driving her crazy. Now she is panic-stricken at the thought that he might leave. She has an unsolvable problem: When he's there physically, he's not there emotionally. The alternative appears to be that he is not there at all. She is a Lion. Her style, worldview, general approach, and responses are dramatically different from his. But we're a long way from ready for my happy little talk about temperament and Lions and Unicorns, and the fact that they seem to always attract and marry one another.

I feel caught in a horrible position. These two people, delightful and attractive as they might be, have waited until the last minute to seek help. This scene can get extremely volatile any moment. What happens in the counseling session might provide hope, or it might prompt one of them to abandon hope and leave.

Theoretically, I'm not supposed to be in a horrible position. I'm a professional. I'm supposed to be therapeutically neutral—which often means I'm not supposed to be real or authentic. I'm supposed to act like a "therapist" instead of as a fully aware, alive human being.

I learned long ago that I can't put on that act. My caring, compassion, and values come out each moment, along with all my pimples and blemishes. And I have found that showing genuine love and being fully present is much more powerful than therapeutic neutrality.

Therapists who got into the field to be "professional" will want to keep a distance. Many have not done a day of personal growth work, have not discovered the "Buddha within," and find the closeness and raw emotion of couples' work extremely threatening. They don't consciously know it's threatening, so they lapse into "neutrality" with its "boundaries" and jargon. These affectations cover the real message to the client, which is, "I am baffled. I haven't done enough personal growth work to meet you where you are. While you're fighting and crying I feel my own stuff coming up inside, and I want to run away."

I know better. I see the pain and the fear in front of me and I know how it makes me feel. And I know how badly I want to help these people get free from their emotional prisons. I also know that I can't do it for them. I can only do what I can from my own awareness, experience, and observations, and pray for a Higher Power to intervene before they blow up their lives. Most importantly, I can't deny my emotional reaction to them: My emotions are sometimes my best tools.

5

While I'm musing over the current dilemma, Pat and Angie lapse back into an argument.

"Okay," I say. "I get the picture. I understand that you both have strong points of view that you want me to hear. But first, I need to get some basic information from you both. Would it be okay if I ask each of you a few questions?"

They nod, and Angie says she is sorry.

As I get my clipboard and paper ready, I think about what I've already heard. They have both given very important clues about what goes on inside of them and why things are not working between them.

Angie's complaint about Pat reveals nothing about Pat but everything about Angie. She claims he will not respond to her. This is his behavior as she sees it—that of not responding. Her interpretation of that behavior is that he "doesn't care" about her. To say this a little differently, Angie has a perceptual lens that makes certain kinds of behavior look like personal attacks when they are not. When Pat does not respond to her, she takes it personally and assumes that he holds her in low regard. This is a Lion's typical way of perceiving. I have seen it in virtually every couple I've ever counseled. But saying that won't help them today.

Pat, too, has revealed tons of information about himself in his short comment. The key to understanding Pat—and all Unicorns, for that matter—is his reference to the word "calm." Calm is a code word for something else. Pat wants Angie's behavior to be calm, for sure. But why? He hasn't referred to an emotion like Angie's "not being cared for." That phrase sounds like feeling unloved, not good enough, or not special. "Calm" doesn't have the same emotional charge. After all, any reasonable person should remain calm, right? So I have to guess Pat's reason for seeking calmness.

Actually, I don't have to guess. I already know what emotion is underneath his need for calm.

"The first thing I want to do," I begin, "is to ask a little bit about your personal history. I thought I might start with you, Pat. Is that okay?"

"Sure, go ahead."

"Good. Before I do the personal history part, though, I want to ask you another question to help me understand something. I noticed you seem to want Angie to be calmer. Could you say what you mean by that?"

"She just gets so out of control, so over the top."

"I do not!" Angie says emphatically. I know this sounds to Pat as if she is starting to get out of control and over the top.

I put up my hand to quiet her. "Angie, I understand you must feel attacked when he says that, but I'm trying to get at something deeper. You noticed he used the phrase "out of control." What do you think he really means by that?"

"He thinks I am an idiot."

"I understand why you would say that. But what if he's saying something more about himself than about you? In other words, when he perceives you going 'out of control,' do you suppose there might be something happening inside of him that has nothing to do with you? What if he is misperceiving what you are doing, and to him it seems out of control? You and I both know that you are in control. So that tells us that something is happening that's not immediately obvious."

Pat is having none of this philosophizing. "No, when she's out of control, she is out of control."

"I understand what you're saying, Pat. Let me ask you, then. When you think she is going out of control, what does that make you want to do in return?"

Pat takes a deep breath and goes silent for a moment. "I guess I just want to get away. I don't like it when she does that."

"That's what he does," Angie pipes up. "He won't talk to me." Her face starts to flush with emotion. "Sometimes he just walks away from me." Her eyes are filling with tears.

"And how does that make you feel?"

"Like he doesn't care about me, like he doesn't want to be with me. I feel rejected." At the word "rejected," my mind goes "Bingo!"

Pat looks on, rolls his eyes, and buries his chin in the palm of his right hand. I gesture toward the ample box of tissue paper so that Angie can dry her tears. Then I wait for what feels like the right moment and continue with Pat.

"So, Pat, about that personal history. Are your parents still alive?"

"My Mom is. My father passed away about ten years ago."

Pat is of medium height with dark brown hair that he passes his fingers through as he talks.

"Do you have brothers and sisters?"

"Yes, an older brother and a younger sister."

"How many years are there between you all?" I ask this question because birth order and the span of years between siblings reveal a lot. These factors set up dynamics in families that are recreated in marriages and work situations. (Yes, it's true that if you're the silent middle child at home you may grow up to be the silent middle manager at work.) It constantly amazes me, though, how resistant people can be to this simple concept. It is widely recognized among psychologists—because it's as easy to spot as a traffic light at an intersection—but the general populace wants to deny it. Nonetheless, our adult lives have huge, deep, and controlling parallels to our early family circumstance.

I once had a female client, for example, who insisted that her anger had nothing whatsoever to do with the way her mother disciplined her. As young as four years old, she experienced the excruciating pain of having her mother shut a cupboard door on her fingers as a regular form of punishment. My office fills up, in fact, with people who have no idea why their life will not work and whose personal history is replete with all forms of cruel abuse. (And we think we live in a civilized society!)

Pat looks like he is mentally counting his fingers and toes. "My brother is five years older than me and my sister is two years younger." There was an emphasis on "brother."

"So he was almost an only child until you came along."

"Yeah, I don't think he was too excited about that—er, me, I mean, coming along when I did."

"Let me see," I muse, "five years. There must not have been sibling rivalry, too many years between you. Possibly sibling disgust?"

"Yeah, you guessed it. I worshiped him. I wanted to follow him everywhere. He never wanted to have anything to do with me."

I ask Pat about his parents. Prior to his father's death, they retired in an RV park somewhere between Warner Springs and Julian in the mountains near Temecula, California. He can't understand why his mother stayed with his father all the years until his death. Dad, like an undocumented army of people, was a rageoholic/alcoholic when Pat was young. His older brother had rebelled against the constant shaming, while Pat had retreated from it.

"I just did my best not to provoke him and to keep a low profile."

"Why did you do that?" I ask innocently even though the answer is obvious. But I want the obvious answer to be stated openly for my own circuitous purposes. I want to use the truth to heal their relationship.

Pat looks at me with momentary incredulity. "Man, he scared me shitless. You never knew what he would do." Yep! There was the emotion I was looking for.

"Was he physically abusive?"

I can almost predict the answer to this question. In my experience, about eight out of ten people who experienced physical abuse as children will see it as normal childrearing.

"Oh, no. My childhood was great. I wasn't abused."

"What about physical discipline then?"

"Oh, there was some of that. Dad had his favorite belt."

"How often did he use it?"

Pat looks up. I know he's visualizing something. Maybe he is counting. "About once a month. But we deserved it. We really got out of line." Pat's eyes are downcast and he's wiggling in his chair.

A recent study showed that one in three boys is physically abused. (So ladies your chances of getting an intact person for a relationship are less than two in three.) Of course that assumes that the adult effects of childhood abuse are obvious. However, two boys experience no physical abuse. What happens to them? Is either of them constantly shamed, criticized, brow-beaten, made to wear girl's clothes, humiliated in public, told he's stupid? If so, which one?

"But I take it that mainly he just yelled."

"Right. Constantly."

And where was Mom when all this was going on?

"Mom just kept to herself. She was depressed for years; at least that was the rumor. I heard she was on some kind medication. She used to sleep a lot. We never talk about that. Anyway she's fine now." Pat sighs and leans back in his chair. "But you know, we all got used to that stuff. It was a pretty good life. We never lacked for anything. Dad was a good provider. Mom kept the home fires burning."

I smile at Pat and thank him for sharing all this with me. I ask a few other questions designed to elicit preliminary information that might be helpful for my understanding of Pat. Nothing else from his background seems to jump out. If it's there, it will emerge later. I can see that Angie has been straining for some time to tell me something.

"Pat and his Dad didn't get along. He didn't tell you that."

"Oh, Angie, my God!" He turns to me to explain. "He was a tyrant and I just learned to stay away from him. That's all."

9

I calm both of them and turn to Angie. "It's your turn."

"Well, my mother is still alive. My father died just two years ago."

"Oh! I'm so sorry. How did he pass away?"

"He died of pancreatic cancer," Angie says. Her eyes are filling with tears. Most people would see that as unresolved grief or the pain still fresh from her loss. I'm seeing something else. Grief and loss, yes; but behind those tears is something much bigger. I'm not thinking about abuse.

"Pancreatic cancer is such a fast, hopeless thing. I'm so sorry. You must have been close to your father to miss him so much," I ask with seeming innocence. But this question also has a hidden motive. I want her to say that she wasn't close to her father. That's the huge well of emotion that's coming up. I sense it clearly in my own emotions. It's her pain, that enormous thing she's carrying around inside of her albeit unacknowledged. I want it on the therapeutic table.

She reaches for my ever-present box of tissues. "I don't know why I'm crying. Dad and I were not close. He was never home. He never did much with the family. He seemed not to want to have much to do with me, or anyone else for that matter."

So there it is—her pain. I could have dinged around for six months without really getting at that. She would have told me about it in a million different ways anyway. The way she looks, the things she says. Embedded in any conversation about relationships will be this thing, this emotional agenda.

My problem is simple. I have a limited amount of time before everything blows up and they go to see their respective lawyers. So I can't sit here with a vacant grin on my face and ask vague questions. I have to stick my finger right into the wound.

Many of my fellow therapists would caution that you must not go too fast or scare the clients. That is true. On the other hand, it's well known that until life hits you square in the forehead with a 2 x 4, you won't "get it"; you will not change, and you will not wake up. So I'm left to strike a delicate balance between a feather and a 2 x 4. It's often not easy to know which is the right one to use.

Angie goes on about her family with very little prompting. She was the oldest of three. Her mother and father worked, and she took care of her younger siblings. Dad traveled a lot. Most important is the emotional picture that emerges as she describes her view of what the family life had been. Mom was hard-working and caring. There wasn't much time for holding, cuddling, or affection. Dad was emotionally unavailable. Theirs was a classic relationship, one that I see often. Her mother was a Lion and her father a Unicorn. As she describes all of this, she uses words like "unloved" and "no one cared for me." These are typical Lion phrases. These are the analogs to Pat's "calm" and "stay away."

In typical Lion fashion, she finishes the story with anger and defiance. She has learned to be strong, she says. "Nobody was going to take care of me but me. So I learned not to count on anyone, but to do it myself." This is another revealing clue as to her internal structure and the way she has patterned her life.

As she finishes giving her personal history, I notice that the hour is about over.

Chapter 2

The Lion and the Unicorn Are in Your Genes

Lions and Unicorns are born, not made. Possibly by now you have figured out where they really come from. Let's look at the metaphors a little more closely, exercising a little poetic license.

The symbol of the Lion is easy to grasp: king of the jungle, hunter, powerful, ferocious, flesh-eater. Lions live in "prides" and are social animals. Even the adult male is affectionate with his own offspring. As affectionate as they are, when they are aroused their roar can be heard more than three miles away. This is a warning to intruders to stay away from their territory. Lions like hunting in the morning when the day is coolest. They are creatures of the sun. They live in grasslands, in sparse forests on the edge of the plains.

Unicorns, on the other hand, are mythical creatures. They are powerful horses, and they have the tail of a lion showing to all that when called on they can fight like a lion. Their fierce-looking yet beautiful horn can be a weapon or an adornment. Unicorns, creatures of the night, live in an enchanted forest hidden by thick stands of trees and overgrown brush. When the moon is full, they may step out into the clearing to commune with other animals that are as gentle as they are. They want someone safe and warm to nuzzle. But they won't allow themselves to be ridden. They bolt and disappear into the forest rather than face open conflict.

Temperament

Temperament is a part of our personality that we get from our biology rather than our social learning. It is Nature vs. Nurture, if you will. Any mother and most fathers can tell within a few weeks of the birth of a second child that he or she is very different from the first-born. This difference is temperament. One good way of thinking about temperament is to see it as something of our personality with which we are born, although this is not strictly true. Prenatal factors such as parental nutrition and drug use can also affect temperament.

Temperament explains the vast differences in how children act and interact with the world around them. Watch children at play for a few minutes. It doesn't take long to see that they have very different approaches to their world. Temperament is a *style of behavior*. Temperament dictates a person's initial *stance* in the world. Objects, people, stimuli, and circumstances all come at us. Our temperament is a genetic blueprint that orients us toward those things and determines how we interact with them.

For parents, the issue of temperament is of paramount importance. Ignoring or misunderstanding a child's temperament can have disastrous consequences. Some children are shy, some are spirited, and some are stubborn. Suppose a family has two children. One's temperament is spirited, adventuresome, and bold while the other is timid, cautious, and shy. Using the same parenting style on both is entirely inappropriate. Each child has dramatically different parenting needs. The bold child needs space to explore and approval for their courage. The timid child needs support and encouragement. Too often exactly the opposite happens: The bold child is restricted and ridiculed and the timid child bullied and terrorized. We will see later that this has disastrous consequences.

Many parents have the mistaken notion that they can mold or "correct" temperament. Traditionally, the thought was that parents could best accomplish this objective through discipline or intimidation. Today we have added an even more insidious tactic—drugs. In our society, it has become in vogue to use medication for "hyperactivity," impulse control, general sedation, and mood improvement. In addition to the widely publicized overuse and misuse of Ritalin, a new generation of children is taking anti-depressants. This less publicized problem is stark and terrifying. Drug companies have not tested these drugs for child use. Moreover, new evidence is revealing that structural changes occur in the adult brain because of taking them. Imagine how much more powerful these are when used with children. Using drugs to treat temperament is malpractice.

Granted, certain combinations of temperament characteristics result in what child psychologists call "the difficult child." Studies have shown that parents of difficult children can experience low self-esteem, a sense of being out of control, and guilt. Nevertheless, the demands of parenthood are not an excuse for ignoring a child's nature when thinking about what is the best fit in terms of approach. As a psychotherapist, I can say with surety that my office is not full of difficult people whose parents had low self-esteem and are guilt ridden because of the challenge of parenting them. It is actually quite the opposite.

Temperament can be broken down into a number of categories, the number of which varies according to the researcher doing the categorization. William Carey, M.D., who wrote *Understanding Your Child's Temperament*, segments temperament into nine compartments: Activity, Regularity, Initial Reaction, Adaptability, Intensity, Mood, Distractibility, Sensitivity, and Persistence and Attention Span (one category). The reason for classifying different aspects of temperament is that no single trait defines an individual. What researchers into child behavior have found is that clusters of temperament traits can be used to categorize children. Temperament, therefore, is one basis on which to develop a profile of a child.

A "shy" child, for example, may be slow to *adapt*, may *initially withdraw*, display less *intensity* and physical *activity*, and have an overall *negative* mood. In this case, the description of the child is a cluster of five temperament categories that give a clearer picture than just labeling the child as "shy." An "easy" child, a "difficult" child, or a "shy" child is a shorthand description of complex combination of traits that makes up a unique and special person.

Let's look at all nine of these traits. Looking at all of them will help orient you to the differences people have right from the start and it will help zero in on the most powerful aspect of temperament that follows all of us right into our most intimate, adult relationships.

Activity

Activity defines the child's penchant for physical activity. Does the child run to you, or wait for you to come to them? Do they run, jump, and tumble, or prefer to amble along? This is the activity part of the temperament spectrum.

Regularity

Some kids get on a schedule and stay on a schedule. Some kids are unpredictable. Regularity is that aspect of temperament that defines how predictable a child is as to sleep, meals, and bodily functions. Regularity defines the rhythms of the child. Are they regular or irregular?

Intensity

Explosive vs. gentle, loud vs. soft—intensity is the level of energy a child uses to express him or herself. This can be for both positive and negative responses. Intensity defines a child as placid on the one hand or vigorous on the other.

Mood

Mood is the overall preference for positive vs. negative emotions. Obviously, every child expresses the entire spectrum of emotions. However, on the continuum from positive to negative, each will land somewhere along the mood scale.

Persistence and Attention Span

A child with high persistence will stick with it. A child with a long attention span will not easily be distracted. These two concepts are really two sides of the same coin.

Distractibility

It is important to note that distractibility is not the opposite of persistence. Distractibility is the way in which a child tunes in or out of his or her surroundings. A child with high persistence is likely to return to a task once the distraction is over.

Sensitivity

Sensitivity in this framework is the amount of stimulation needed for a child to notice it. This is different from distractibility. Sensitivity describes a child's threshold to awareness of what is going on around them.

Adaptability

This aspect of temperament is related to but should not be confused with the next category of "initial reaction." Adaptability refers to how easy or difficult it is for a child to change his or her initial reaction in desirable ways given the social situation. A child with low adaptability may have to "warm up" before joining group activities, for instance.

Initial Reaction

I saved the most interesting for last. Lions and Unicorns have differing clusters of temperament traits. Initial reaction is the most interesting because this is where the most obvious difference between Lions and Unicorns shines through. To understand "initial reaction," however, there is another term we must understand, since this takes us into formal research on infants. The term is "arousal." Arousal is a term that means stimulation, excitement, or to be stirred. We can be sexually aroused. We can be aroused from sleep. Arousal in turn leads to two more terms that are formal: "approach" and "withdrawal."

One question that intrigues researchers about children is: when aroused do they approach or withdraw? It turns out that some approach and some withdraw. We are each born with a preference for either approach or withdrawal, and that is the concept of importance to our discussion. This preference, like all inborn traits, exists on a continuum. In other words, not all of us when aroused approach or withdraw with the same alacrity.

Arousal and the Brain

Now we need to take a look at the how our brains set our basic patterns in motion before we have any clue of what's going on. It turns out that the brains of people who prefer survival strategies that involve approach, attack, predatory activity, etc., are noticeably different than the brains of people who incline toward survival strategies of withdrawal, avoidance, seeking safety, shutting up, and shutting down. Seeing how these knee-jerk types of biological responses disposes us one way or another really does help us gain some freedom in how we act.

We can think of the brain as divided into three parts. Some have characterized these parts in evolutionary terms as the lizard brain, the mammalian brain, and the human brain. These three categories relate to their physical depth inside the brain as well as how they relate to our survival.

The lizard brain, or brain stem and lower parts of the brain, controls all of the automatic functions related to how we stay alive: body temperature, heart rate, and breathing. In other words, it controls the functions that keep our body alive. The next part of the brain, sometimes called the mammalian brain, is the Limbic System. Deep inside the brain, this collection of sub-parts controls how we keep ourselves safe in the outside world. It is the storehouse of all of our automatic survival tactics. The Limbic System includes the Amygdala, the Hippocampus, and a number of other primitive structures. If we widen our view of the "mammalian brain" just a bit, we include the *midbrain*, which includes the Thalamus and Cingulate Gyrus.

The entire midbrain, including the Limbic System, is a primitive part of the brain located deep inside. In essence, its job is to keep us from being part of the food chain, which was entirely appropriate and necessary for our hunter-gatherer forbearers. For them, an automatic response to a threat or the sight of prey was essential. The system of responses that evolved then consisted of strategies most appropriate to ensure survival. The cornerstone of survival in this framework is "arousal," which informs us how to respond when something new happens.

When we are "aroused," the level of arousal emanates from a part of the brain called the Locus Ceruleus. The actual input itself (except for our sense of smell) flows to the Thalamus for initial processing. The Thalamus and the Locus Ceruleus then signal the Amygdala, which processes the emotional content of input. You might wonder about the sense of smell. It interfaces directly with the Amygdala. The Amygdala, then, is like Grand Central Station for emotions.

Once the Amygdala processes the emotions, the Hippocampus gets into the act by checking memory for similar instances of emotion and historical circumstances. The meaning of this comparison modulates the stream of information, which travels to the orbit frontal or prefrontal cortex, the brain's planning and problem-solving center. The prefrontal lobes along with the rest of the cerebral cortex function as the "third" part of the brain, the "human brain." I also refer to the prefrontal lobes as the "adult brain." More often than not; tragically, the adult brain just passes all of the information on to the Hypothalamus for an automatic response.

The Hypothalamus' job is to activate the HPA axis, the Hypothalamic/ Pituitary/Adrenal axis. The HPA axis modulates the release of strong brain chemicals and hormones. One of these chemicals released by the action of the HPA axis is norepinepherine. The effects of norepinepherine on the body include increased focus, attention, and alertness; increase in short term memory; increases in pupil dilation and awareness of peripheral vision; as well as adjustment in skeletal muscle tone.

Depending on the level of arousal, we prepare for flight or fight. Predators go into a *fight* state of readiness and prey go into a *flight* state of readiness. As strange as it may seem, some of us have primitive brains

17

predisposed to being prey and some predisposed to be predators. This is our "initial reaction."

Obviously, all of us have the capability of being either predator or prey if the situation calls for it. At some level many animals are either eating or being eaten so the roles of predator and prey are versatile roles. In one circumstance, a rat is prey for an owl; in another, the rat is attacking a smaller varmint. How does one decide which to be?

The role of the Prefrontal Cortex and the Hippocampus are the key. Higher order functions of the brain that allow us to analyze and plan, along with our memory of historical experiences, serve as a road map for our perception of what is happening to us. We must create meaning in order to become predator or prey. Nevertheless, experiments with children show a preference for approach or withdrawal. *Approach* or *withdrawal* may seem very different from *predator* or *prey*; and it is. The basic neurological equipment, however, is the same.

Approach/Withdrawal

There is yet another system of the brain that goes into action when we are aroused. But what goes into action varies according to our preference for approach or withdrawal. Research has shown that those who prefer to approach activate the left frontal area of the brain, which facilitates fine motor behavior, language, and the expression of certain positive emotions. Activation of the left frontal area has also recently been shown to be related to the expression of anger whose purpose is to overcome some external obstacle. In contrast, those of us who prefer to withdraw when our Central Nervous System is aroused activate the right frontal area of the brain. This prepares this individual to activate gross motor movements, autonomic reactivity, and the expression of negative affects. Researchers believe that these biological preferences bias an individual's interactions with the outside world such that some may initiate while others may withdraw from stressful or unfamiliar social exchanges.

Studies confirm these facts in repeatedly using EEG (electroencephalograph) tests, which show frontal brain wave asymmetries between infants. The implication of this phenomenon is profound: It offers physical support for the notion that, as I stated in the opening paragraph of this chapter, *Lions and Unicorns are born, not made!* How does the brain of a child know it is a Lion or a Unicorn? Scientists speculate that these preferences arise in the brain stem of the human embryo, which then regulates asymmetries in development and in the functioning of the cerebral cortex.

But wait there's more! Even when we are not "aroused" it seems that Lions and Unicorns have another basic biological difference. Lions have a bias toward activating the Sympathetic Nervous System while Unicorns prefer activation of the Parasympathetic Nervous System. An easy way to visualize this is to imagine the heart beating. The SNS want to excite us and would drive the heart to beat faster. The PSN wants to inhibit us and slows down the heart beat. In fact, if you watch the heart beating in real time, you will see what's called heart rate variability HRV.

When we take our heart rate, we count a certain number of beats and divide by a certain number of seconds. That only gives us an average of say 70 beats per minute. In reality the heart is dancing constantly around 70 beats per minute. The SNS pushes it faster and the PSN pulls it slower. This push-pull shows up in a rather jagged waveform that represents the constant struggle between the SNS and the PNS.

In this same way the SNS pushes us to more excitement and activation and the PNS pulls us toward inhibition – one moving us toward the world and the other away from the world. Thus, the internal regulating system of a Lion is biased to a predominance of Sympathetic excitement whereas the internal regulating system of the Unicorn is biased toward Parasympathetic inhibition.

This all may seem a little complicated, so let's just go back to the bottom line: Brains are different. There appear to be two basic types of brains: those that facilitate and prefer approach, attack, predatory, exploratory functions, and self-preserving strategies; and those that facilitate withdrawal, avoidance, safe-seeking, shutting-up, and shutting-down strategies for self-preservation.

Here are some key points to remember throughout this book.
1. We are genetically predisposed to become Lions or Unicorns.
2. Stress lights up the Lion's left frontal lobe and the Unicorn's right frontal lobe.
3. The Amygdala is the center for emotional reactions.
4. The Hippocampus is the nexus for pairing our current experience with previous experience. In other words, our perception emerges from this primitive part of the brain.

5. The adult brain is "in the loop" since the orbital frontal cortex is connected directly with the Limbic System.

The Lion and Unicorn Temperaments

Just as a person's total temperament is as a cluster of different aspects of temperament, the Lion and Unicorn model fits the same philosophy. We can easily go back through many of the individual categories of temperament and see how some are more Lion qualities while others are more Unicorn qualities. We can also see that each person is an individual and is not so easy to categorize.

Initial reaction does have the most consistent fit with the metaphors of the Lion and the Unicorn. There is one caution however. The Lion temperament and the Unicorn temperament are directly involved with how we view relationships with others of our own kind. Approach/withdrawal is not restricted to just that context. We may see inconsistencies. For instance, I remember being extremely shy when it came to girls when I was a schoolboy, but in relationships I am definitely a Lion. I have clients who are Unicorns who consistently displayed "approach" preferences as children. The Lion and Unicorn are models that, to the extent they are a match, will help us understand the dance of the relationships, the underlying dynamics, emotions, and motivations.

Gender Roles

Two problems arise as we discover who we are. Cultural stereotypes tell us that Lions should be men and Unicorns should be women. One such cultural myth has men living on one planet and women living on another. Some of us are desperate for a rocket ship that will take us to the other planet.

Male participants who come to my Lion/Unicorn workshop are often chagrined to discover that they are Unicorns. Yet some large percentage (I estimate about half) of all men are Unicorns. No man wants to see himself as weak, helpless, or effeminate. The Unicorn type is anything but those qualities. We will see later that Unicorns employ a passive defense. We will also see that even passivity is a massive exercise of personal power, cunning, and will. This is not weakness at all. In fact, in mythology the Unicorn was actually more powerful than the Lion. The Unicorn was the most powerful creature in existence.

It turns out that about half of the women I see are Lions. Often society labels these women as having "male energy." That is unfortunate. Later we will see that Lions use an active defense. This is no more "male" than a Unicorn is female.

The Lion and Unicorn temperaments do not track gender. As many women are Lions as are Unicorns. Men exhibit in the same proportion as well. Cultural stereotypes are an easy way to label people without getting to know and respect them. The Lion and Unicorn model is a way of understanding personal interactions, not a way of disrespecting differences.

Adult Temperament Models

How does all this fit with popular models of adult temperament? The most popular measurement of adult temperament in use today is the Myers-Briggs Type Indicator. David Keirsey popularized this measure for our generation in his groundbreaking books *Please Understand Me* and *Please Understand Me II*.

This school of thought sorts individuals into 16 different categories according to their tendency toward four differing choices: introversion vs. extraversion, intuition vs. sensation, thinking vs. feeling, and judging vs. perceiving. Let's explore these differences.

You are an introvert if you rehearse your communication before you say it. Oftentimes you may have to tell someone who is waiting for a response that you are still "processing." Extraverts, in contrast, are spontaneous communicators. They open their mouths before they think.

Moving to the next grouping, intuitives have their head in the clouds. They are the dreamers, the thinkers of the possibilities. Sensing or sensation-seeking folks, in contrast, have their feet planted firmly on the ground. They want the facts. They want the facts in concrete terms, and the more facts the better.

Thinking vs. feeling is easy to distinguish. When presented with a problem, thinkers go immediately to their head while feelers go to their heart.

Judges and perceivers are terms that are not particularly helpful in describing these traits. Let us just say that judges have strong opinions, like deadlines, and closure. Perceivers are laid back, see both sides of the issues, and can let it ride. Judges organize life while perceivers let life organize them.

Reality Takes an Unexpected Turn from Theory

As an assiduous student of Keirsey, I incorrectly thought that the Lion and the Unicorn equated, respectively, with introversion and extroversion. This came to me as a "great revelation." There turned out to be three problems, however, with this theory. First, according to Keirsey's research, only 25% of all of us are introverts while 75% are extroverts. Hmmm! When I did the math, that meant that 25% of extroverts would never get married since more often than not a Lion marries a Unicorn. Clearly, the numbers were not working in favor of my theory.

The next knotty little issue was that Keirsey himself devotes some time in his latest book discussing Jung's as well as Briggs' confusion of introversion with intuition and extroversion with sensation. He then organizes the entire book such that introversion/extraversion is a subtype of dimensions of personality. He sees the root of these traits as related to the use of Tools vs. Words, an argument that left me a bit uneasy.

These are small issues compared to the most compelling evidence that introversion vs. extraversion is not the path to relational enlightenment. I was horrified to find Lions appearing in my office who were introverts. Arggh! Then I discovered extraverted Unicorns. My God, the world turned upside down. Then I noticed couples made up of an extraverted Unicorn and an introverted Lion!

Clearly, the Lion and the Unicorn did not spring out of the whole cloth of the Myers-Briggs Type Indicator. I had to look elsewhere. The search for the answer led me to childhood temperament and approach/withdrawal.

At this point, I knew one amazing fact. Nearly all of the couples I saw were a Lion and a Unicorn together. I could tie their interactions to temperament rather than to some pathology. I could also conclude that we are attracted in some fashion to our opposite type. It was a start—a foundation. If that was true and so natural, though, then why are so many marriages and relationships in trouble?

Chapter 3

Pat and Angie Discover Their Child Brains

Darwin Can't Handle His Wife's Anger

Darwin has seen me five times before and now is staring at me as I respond to what he's telling me. He originally came because he wasn't handling his wife's anger well. It seems that she yells as a normal form of communication with him and their two small children. As a result, their little girl shows aggressive behavior with her brother and other children. He has just informed me that his pastor no longer wants him to come to me because, according to her, I'm not right with God. The pastor says that Darwin's wife must pray for healing. That will stabilize the relationship.

I run into this from time to time when I encounter fundamentalist Christians. Freud thought he had uncovered all of the psychological defenses. He evidently never had a client who was a fundamentalist. "The Jesus Defense" is what I call it. As soon as someone thinks their cover will be blown, they use the Jesus Defense. They don't have to take responsibility; they don't have to look deeply into their feelings or motives; and don't have to look at their own stuff, because Jesus will do it for them. Jesus will heal them; if they need to know about it, Jesus will show them. Of course, if I assault their psychological defenses in any way that means that I am not right with Jesus.

Never mind that Jesus, Paul, Peter, and John went through years and many trials before they were ready to preach the word of God. Never mind that psychological health intertwines with spiritual maturity.

Darwin seems to be struggling with a dilemma. Should he continue to see me or listen to his pastor, who is clearly plugged in to the Almighty in a way he cannot fathom?

"I've got to keep coming to you, Doc. If I don't, I'm going to hurt her. I swear, if she doesn't stop shouting and yelling, I'm going to do property damage."

Here we get into that "Unicorns are more powerful than Lions" idea discussed in the last chapter. Unicorns don't see themselves as angry. They don't like being around anger. They get resentful. However, resentment will build and build until it explodes. That's what Darwin is talking about. He is a Unicorn on the verge of exploding, and he knows the damage he will do when it happens.

I like clients like Darwin. He is a contractor, so he pays in cash. And he is a man, so I can tell him pretty much anything I want: He has to take it because he is a man and men have to take it like a man. That's the man code.

"That Jesus stuff is a red herring, Darwin. You know that—or have I misjudged you? You know her behavior with the children is just short of the kind of verbal abuse I have to report to the Department of Children's Services."

He looks at me with a mixture of panic and exasperation. "I just don't think I can take it any more. I mean, I know God wants me to stay with her because of the children and all. But why do I have to be with another crazy woman? Every woman I have ever been with has been crazy."

"Darwin," I say, trying to get his undivided attention, "you can focus on the crazy women all you want and you'll never get your answer. The answer is inside of you."

I can tell he isn't hearing me. He's listening to the screaming inside his head—her screaming. His wife is probably a Borderline (on the fence right between psychosis and neurosis), which means she alternates between psychotic rage and panicky fear of abandonment. His life is probably a living hell. But he is responsible for his own hell, and half of her anger is his anger being projected onto her. Unfortunately, he is light-years in a spaceship away from ever understanding that!

He's still murmuring something about his wife's behavior being overwhelming to him. I have to restrain myself as I want to get up, go over to him, and shake him violently.

"Darwin, listen to me. Remember the first day you came in here?"

He shakes his head yes.

"Do you remember how you prayed and asked God for help?"

"Yeah," he says, "and I opened the yellow pages with my eyes closed and I pointed, and there was your picture."

"Right," I say and lean forward, hoping to fill his field of view. "God is giving you the answer you prayed for. I'm the answer. I'm telling you: You *must* stop looking at your wife and focus on yourself."

"Yeah, but what would you do if your wife was raging all the time? One minute it's great and the next minute, out of the clear blue, she's angry and throwing things. She needs help. I think she's mentally ill."

I take another deep breath and start again. "Darwin, you're probably right. But she isn't 'here. You are. We can't fix her. We can only fix you. We can spend my time and your money focusing on her and her defects, or we can work on something we have some control over—you!"

Darwin isn't ready to focus on himself. He just wants to complain about her, and I'm bullheaded enough not to let him off the hook. My chances of helping him are slim, but I have to try. He knows how hard I'm pulling for him, even if he isn't ready to hear what I'm saying. That's my one redeeming quality: I can establish rapport and disarm people. He knows I care even if I piss him off a little.

As he leaves, he gives me an extra $20. I know he's really paying it to God. It's like an extra tithe. He thinks that if he gives the Lord a little more in the offering plate, the Lord will help him. If he keeps doing that, I know that at least I will.

Pat and Angie's System of Interlocking Reactivity

Pat and Angie have been in the waiting room just a few moments as Darwin leaves. They usher themselves in and we exchange pleasantries. They say they are glad they're coming to counseling. They finally are doing something positive in their relationship, they say. They appear to be eager to go on to the next step, whatever that may be.

25

I spend the first half of the session explaining the concept of the Lion and Unicorn. They seem mildly interested and readily agree that Angie is the Lion and Pat is the Unicorn.

They're a little shocked when I tell them that nearly every couple I see is a Lion matched with a Unicorn.

"Are you ready to see your relationship the way I see it?"

Angie pipes up, "Oh, yes, please!" Pat doesn't look quite so enthusiastic. That's typical of a Unicorn. They hold back most of themselves most of the time.

I spoke once to a group of about 60 men. I explained the Lion/Unicorn concept, and as I finished I turned to them and asked, "So, how many of you think you are Lions?" About half of the men raised their hands.

I nodded and asked, "And how many of you are Unicorns?" No hands, not one went up. There was an embarrassing moment as the Lions look around the room and then questioningly toward me.

I smiled and said, "You didn't think they would actually raise their hands did you?" With that, the entire room broke into laughter. The Unicorns knew I had busted their cover and the entire group vividly got the point.

I ask Pat and Angie if they would mind if I drew it out on the whiteboard that covers one wall of my office. They respond positively and I pick up the black marker and jump to my feet. I draw two large circles, one on the left and one on the right. The one on the left I label "Pat" and the one on the right I label "Angie."

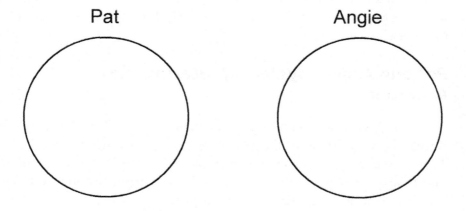

Figure 3-1 Pat and Angie's System—part A

"Okay. If we're going to talk about a relationship, we better have both people on the board. Now there's no right place to start here. So I'm going to start with Angie. Angie, when Pat won't respond to you or just walks away as you told me last time, how does that make you feel?"

She begins to tear up, but I hold up my hand and she immediately understands that this is an exercise in reflecting rather than acting something out. "I feel like he doesn't care."

"Okay. And Pat, when Angie gets angry and you walk away, what feeling do you have?"

"I don't know really. I just want to get out of there."

This doesn't surprise me. Unicorns have a particular problem. Since their defense is *avoiding,* they shut down their feelings. In a way, I'm asking a very threatening question. I want him to feel a feeling. He is all about disconnecting from his feelings. This may take some time. Angie, on the other hand, may not be aware of her feelings, but Lions don't deny their feelings or hide from them. Generally, Lions can identify their feelings much more easily than Unicorns.

At first, it may seem from my point of view that Lions are easier to work with than Unicorns. To an extent that's true. It's much easier to get a Lion to take responsibility for his or her entire defensive structure. Unicorns often find that step in therapy the hardest. I've had Unicorns sit in my office for months and never understand what I was asking them, because it was so threatening for them to acknowledge that they have painful emotions.

This seems all neat and tidy in favor of Lions being successful in therapy. Au, contraire, mon ami. There is a grave danger of emotionally triggering a Lion in session. It might be the last time you see them as they slam the door on their way out.

"Pat, I know I'm asking a difficult question. But what is the feeling that makes you want to avoid or escape when Angie gets angry?" I watch him struggling with the answers, so I offer: "In other words, what's the first thought that goes through your mind?"

Pat thinks for a moment and then says. "I don't know. I'm just drawing a blank."

"Pat, I want you to know that that's fine. 'Drawing a blank' means that something significant is happening inside of you. Let me ask you a different question. Would that be okay?"

"Sure." Pat looks as if he is very uncomfortable.

I'm about to shift his focus in a way that I hope will change his perception of what's happening. My experience tells me that the defense of avoiding is usually operating. In other words, the reason Pat can't access the information that I'm asking him for is the same reason that he walks away from Angie. The same defensive structure that causes him to run, avoid, or escape is creating the "blank" he experiences as I talk to him.

"Pat, when I ask you a question like, 'What are you feeling?' what happens inside of you?"

"I'm not sure I understand."

"Here I am, asking you a very difficult question about your feelings. What happens to you when I ask it?"

Pat squirms in his chair a little and then his face brightens. "I feel very uncomfortable."

I exclaim, "Right!" I'm so excited I can hardly contain it. Why am I so excited? Because to answer the question, he had to feel the feeling. I know that it's the same feeling that he always feels. It's the same feeling that makes him flee from Angie. It's a feeling that he has run from all his life.

"Can you describe that uncomfortable feeling? Where is it in your body?"

Pat points to just below his sternum.

"Keep your hand right there and feel the feeling. Do you feel it?"

"Yeah, it doesn't feel good."

"No, Pat, it doesn't," I agree. "Now take some time and analyze the feeling. See if you can label it."

"I feel bad. It's a bad feeling."

"Okay, can you be a little more descriptive? Pretend that I don't know what 'bad' really means. Here I'm asking you this probing question and you're getting a bad feeling. What does *bad* feel like right there in your gut?"

"Could it be nervousness? It feels like I'm nervous."

I'm rejoicing to myself. Great, he labeled the feeling! Probably for the first time in his adult life, he's having the experience of knowing what experience he's having. I ask him, "Could 'anxious' be another word for it?"

"Yeah, nervous, anxious—just kind of overwhelmed."

"Great! Now let me ask another question. Is it the question I'm asking you that makes you nervous, or the fact that I'm asking you a question at all?"

Pat grins at me. "I don't even remember the question. So I guess just being asked a question makes me nervous."

"What are you afraid might happen?"

Pat's answer is more confident now. He's figuring out where I'm coming from. "I'm afraid that I might give you the wrong answer."

I formulate another leading question, hoping that the chain of aware answers will continue. "I'm going to ask another question. When you hear it, just answer with the first thing that pops into your mind—even if it makes no sense. Okay?"

"Go ahead."

"If you answer the question wrong, what do you think might happen?"

"You'll get angry!" he blurts out. Then he looks at me quizzically.

I let the room get quiet. Then I ask in a soft voice, "Pat, look deep inside. There is an angry face looking at you. Who is it?"

"My father," he says in almost a whisper as a tear forms in the corners of his eyes.

This entire time, Angie has sat in rapt silence watching the interaction between Pat and me. She seems to know the significance of what has just happened. I let silence settle in over the three of us.

I become aware of birds singing outside, and I can hear the meditation music coming from my waiting room. I imagine I hear the gurgling of the little fountain that sits amidst the magazines on the table there.

When the moment is right, I finally speak. "So is it fair to say, Pat, that when Angie gets angry, you get this real nervous, anxious feeling inside?"

He nods, still a little stunned as to what has been happening. I get up and walk to the whiteboard and draw two more circles:

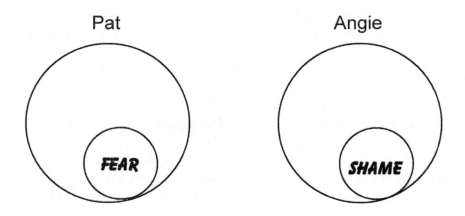

Figure 3-2 Pat and Angie's System—part B

"Now, inside Angie is a part that carries the pain of 'nobody cares.' Remember, Angie, you said that's the feeling you get whenever Pat avoids you?"

"Right, but why have you labeled it 'shame'?"

"Ah, good question. I use the term 'shame' because it's a more general term. But feeling like nobody cares is reflective of a global sense of not being loved, accepted, and approved, etcetera. That feeling is a feeling of shame. But it's important that you use the term that most closely matches your experience. Right now, that term is a feeling of 'nobody cares.'"

I gesture to Pat. "Now Pat has a part of him that experiences lots of fear. Fear is just another word for the nervousness or anxiety that we talked about a few minutes ago. This doesn't mean that Pat is fearful or a coward in any sense. This is more a feeling of being overwhelmed—a kind of 'Here we go again' sort of feeling."

Pat speaks up. "*Here we go again.* That's exactly what goes through my mind when Angie starts to get angry. Here we go again."

"Right," I say. "Like here comes an ordeal. Oh my God, I've got to go through this again!"

"That's it exactly."

"Okay, excellent." I turn back to the board and point to the "fear." "So, Pat, when you get that 'Here we go again' feeling, you try to avoid the conflict, don't you—by avoiding or not responding, right?"

He nods and I draw another circle on the board. "And, Angie, when Pat avoids you, it feels like he doesn't care and you get angry. So there is this angry part inside of you, isn't there?"

"You bet!"

Now my picture looks like this.

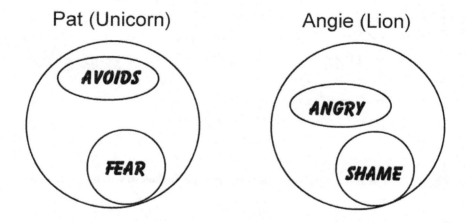

Figure 3-3 Pat and Angie's System—part C

"Now watch what happens." I take my black marker and start drawing lines. "When Angie gets angry, Pat feels fear, 'Here we go again.' He then tries to *avoid* the conflict. When he does this, Angie thinks, 'So, he doesn't care about me.' Then Angie gets angry and around and around we go."

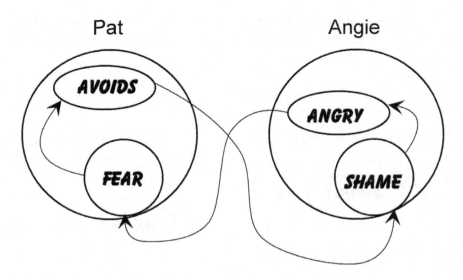

Figure 3-4 Pat and Angie's Limbic Systems Interlocked in Circular Causality

Pat and Angie's jaws drop. She says, "My God, that's our relationship."

"Right, and since it's circular, we could have started at any point in the circle. In other words, all four parts of you involved are equally responsible for what's not working in the relationship."

Pat pipes up, "I can see that is exactly what happens. How do we change it?"

"I'm glad you asked that question. In order to change it, you need more information. First, you need to know what the black circle is. I haven't really told you yet. You probably assumed that I meant the black circles to represent the whole person." Pat and Angie nod, and I continue, "Actually, this black circle is a part of your brain called the Limbic System. It's the part of the brain that's fully developed by the time you're three to five years old. I call it 'the child brain.' Let me draw in the rest of the brain."

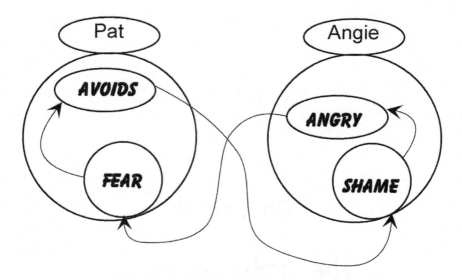

Figure 3-5 Pat and Angie's whole brain

I tell them that the top circle with their names in it is the "adult brain." The problem with their relationship is that the child brain, the Limbic System, has been running their relationship. The purpose behind marriage counseling is going to be to put the adult brains in charge. They seemed interested and willing to come back again and work further on this. One can only hope.

Chapter 4

The Limbic System—
Lizards Dream of Relationships

Here's a news flash: *YOU HAVE THREE BRAINS!*

Looks like the headline from one of those supermarket tabloids, doesn't it? The fact is that we have three distinct brain structures in our heads—each in its own way like a complete and independent brain. The oldest "brains," in evolutionary terms, physically lie underneath the newest brains.

Scientists call the deepest or lowest brain the "primitive" or "reptilian brain." I call it the "lizard" brain. It is made up of the brain stem, the pons, the cerebellum, the olfactory bulbs, and some other old slimy stuff. Famed neuroscientist Paul MacLean dubbed this latter the "R-complex."

The lizard brain is responsible for keeping us alive. It helps us breathe, digest, reproduce, and smell, and it operates some of our involuntary reflexes. When I think of a lizard, I think of only three activities: appearing catatonic, laying an egg, and killing something by devouring it in the blink of an eye with a lethal, quick tongue. That description fits some couples in my practice perfectly: Sometimes I suspect they kill their young.

Ah, yes, even lizards dream of relationships. That's where the next brain comes in. This is the Limbic System, often called the mammalian brain. I've also heard it referred to as the "mid-brain." To repeat and expand on points introduced in chapter two, the Limbic System corresponds to the brain of most of the lower carnivores and herbivores such as cats and dogs and wildebeests. We'll discuss it more later in this chapter.

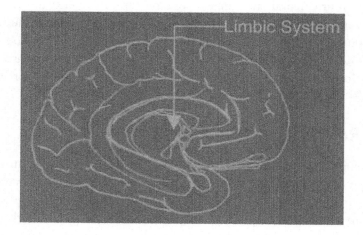

Figure 4-1 The Limbic System is deep inside the brain.

Notice in the diagram that the Limbic System is deep in the center of the brain. The next picture shows the various structures of the Limbic System, which comes complete with a "cap" called the Cingulate Gyrus. Just above that structure is the Cerebral Cortex, which is part of the third brain. It looks a little like a Cap on a cap. This is the "new mammalian" brain. We humans share this structure with only the most advanced primates.

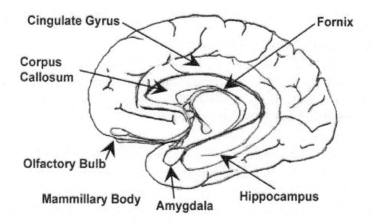

Figure 4-2 The structures of the Limbic System

Here we have three brains, each distinct but interconnected. Incredibly, each brain or cerebral layer appears one on top of the next in succession during embryo and fetal development. This recreates the evolutionary development of humankind from lizards to *homo sapiens*. In an odd way, this also is an allegory for marriage counseling. The goal of counseling is to transform lizards or enraged rhinos (lions and unicorns) into something equivalent to Cro-Magnon.

The Role of the Limbic System

Survival. That's the key word to remember when evaluating the function of the Limbic System. While the lizard brain helps us stay alive physically and instinctively, the Limbic System helps us survive as part of the food chain. It helps us know when to flee like prey or fight like a predator. The unique role of this part of the brain is to add in the emotional content of our everyday experience.

Emotions or feelings tell us what is agreeable and what is disagreeable. Emotions such as anger, fear, lust, love, joy, and sadness originate in the mammalian brain. In addition, memory is a unique aspect of the Limbic System.

To put it all into a simple idea: *This part of the brain is for learning to survive by using emotions and memory.* It is a warehouse of our strategies for how to deal with the basic situations of life without "thinking." That's right! The Limbic System's job is to take care of us without involving the higher functions of the brain. It is automatic, self-preserving, and reactive.

Early Childhood Development

There has been a lot of talk lately about "early childhood development." Why is that? Quite simply, it's because the first three years of life are the most critical ones. If things go wrong during those years, a person's life may never get back on "track." Meeting critical needs such as nutrition, security, attachment, and stability is essential during this stage of development.

What do those needs have to do with the Limbic System? That's the only part of the brain in full development during the first three years. The Cerebral Cortex is certainly involved also, in terms of learning to walk and talk. But the Prefrontal Lobes, behind the forehead where the adult decision-making brain resides, don't really start getting wired up until we're about five years old, and their development isn't complete until we're in high school. Meanwhile, the Limbic System is completely developed and fully wired up by the time we're three to five.

An easy way to tell the difference between the Limbic System and the Prefrontal Lobes is to ask a five year-old which is heavier, a pound of feathers or a pound of coal. The answer you get will nearly always be "a pound of coal." To answer the question correctly, the child must be able to link the intangible concept of a "pound" with the concrete object of coal or feathers. Psychology calls the facility needed to do this "formal operations."

The primitive brain of a child can easily distinguish the properties of different objects: Pillows are soft, rocks are hard, dogs bark, and cats meow. But linking concepts with objects is something the child simply does not yet have the mental power to do. Ask adolescents the same question and you'll get the right answer, because their cortex has enough neural connections to bridge the developmental gap. Ask a teenager the same question and they'll say, "That's a trick question."

Limbic System learning is subject to a lot of literal, magical thinking, as well as to many broad generalizations about the child's world. Since no critical thinking can take place, distinctions about events, assumptions about relationships, and trying to ascertain who is to blame or responsible for bad experiences in the world create cognitive distortions and beliefs that are imprinted in the child's rapidly developing brain.

How rapidly is the child's brain developing? A two year-old has about 20 times as many neural connections operating as a forty-two year-old does. These neural nets are the stuff of learning, and these connections form and are pruned at a furious pace. Imagine the massive learning it takes for a child to take his or her first step. Imagine the kind of neural development that has to happen for a child to learn to talk. Imagine the neural development needed for a child to form a relationship with another person.

Attachment

The first few years of human life are called the "attachment phase." During this phase, bonding must occur for the child to survive. A child not held and attended to develops a condition called "failure to thrive." The child loses weight and literally shrivels away. If the bonding process is chaotic, unreliable, or abusive, the child develops adaptations that interfere with relationships throughout his or her entire lifetime. If the developing brain receives no stimulation it doesn't learn, and the child grows up with enormous cognitive deficits.

Attachment experiences condition the Limbic System. Scientists now know, for example, that abuse and stress during this critical period literally alter the structure of the Limbic System. In all probability, the seeds for personality disorders and trauma-based mental illnesses such as disassociation-type disorders are sown during this time. This is not to say that the years immediately after the attachment phase are not also fertile ground for the formation of neurosis and psychosis in response to abuse; however, the earlier the abuse occurs, the more intractable are the mental consequences.

Children with attachment deficits grow up to be adults whose emotions are out of control. They have fits of rage, and periods of uncontrollable and inconsolable sadness. They display irrational jealousy and have no trust. They present themselves as victims and act as perpetrators. They become hermits. They drift from job to job and from relationship to relationship. Often they are in and out of the social services system. The cost to society of poor attachment is direct and staggering.

The Amygdala and Hippocampus

The Amygdala and Hippocampus tell us all we need to know about the function of the Limbic System. As mentioned in chapter two, the Amygdala is Grand Central Station for emotions. The Hippocampus is responsible for pairing the incoming information, level of arousal, and emotional input with similar circumstances in memory.

Abuse and stress during early childhood development causes the Amygdala to get *inflamed,* for lack of a better term. These experiences alter its structure in a way that makes the person far more emotionally sensitive and reactive than what we consider the norm. Meanwhile these same experiences cause the Hippocampus to become smaller, which causes a reduction in the ability to remember.

All of this puts the child into a state of hypervigilance and hyperarousal, which produces lifelong symptoms of Post Traumatic Stress Disorder, PTSD. This means that throughout the lifespan, the behavior of others is misinterpreted and will trigger extreme emotional reactions. Because of alterations that have occurred in the Amygdala (causing over-arousal) and the Hippocampus (resulting in reduced memory), the person reacts compulsively to certain kinds of perceptions and cannot remember why. This is due to the alterations that have occurred in the Amygdala causing over-arousal, and reductions in the structure of the Hippocampus resulting in reduced memory. In the case of anger, for example, you're pissed off, but you can't remember why.

Just beyond Attachment

The American psychoanalyst Erik Erikson made major contributions to the field of psychology with his work on child development and identity crisis. He is most famous for codifying stages of human development. The first four pairs in his model are trust vs. mistrust, autonomy vs. shame, initiative vs.guilt, and industry vs. inferiority. His reasoning was that if a person doesn't pass successfully through one or more stages of development as a child, that person can end up with lifelong issues involving mistrust, shame, guilt, or inferiority, or all of the above, or some of the above, or none of the above. Looking at the left term in each stage, normal development progresses from trust to autonomy to initiative to industry. One gets the feeling that children move out of the attachment phase (trust), discover themselves as separate from the mother (autonomy), then from three to six years of age start seeing themselves as in a relationship to which they bring their own identity and contribution (initiative and industry). In fact, after attachment at around age five, the adult brain, specifically the prefrontal lobes, starts wiring up. The child for the first time can "look at themselves" in relationship to someone else. With the advent of the frontal lobes, some primitive self-referencing or self-observation is possible. Children can then start measuring their value as a person separate from someone else in their world.

Whereas the attachment object is nearly always the mother, or whoever is nearby consistently during the first three years, now the child picks out someone with whom to be in relationship. My experience is that this can be either the mother or father. This process does not track gender. Girls as well as boys will pick either parent for their "relationship." Because of this developmental step, an imprint etches a pattern of what a relationship is, and how to survive it, in the neural nets connected to the reactive, automatic, self-preserving brain. What happens next is called "splitting."

Parts

There is a mental condition called DID, Dissociative Identity Disorder. We used to call it multiple personality disorder or MPD. The story of how someone gets this disorder is not pretty. It is tragic and the result of extreme childhood abuse. What happens in the developing brain of the child is that the stress and emotions produced by experiencing the abuse split off into sub-personalities designed to cope with and compartmentalize the trauma.

Just as we now know that stress alters Limbic Structures, we also know that stress at some point will cause the brain to adapt by splitting off "parts." Discussing DID and its causes is beyond the scope of this book and rather distasteful. The depth of human depravity knows no bounds. Large numbers of children are ritualistically tortured, and physically and sexually abused in horrific ways. DID is the result.

It occurred to me that this splitting phenomenon might be a natural response of the Limbic System rather than a maladaptive response. In other words, we contain multiple personalities. The natural function of the Limbic System is to create parts or sub-personalities to deal with various emotional responses and social adaptations made in the normal course of development. DID is a more extreme example of that adaptation, such that the splitting is more complete and compartmentalized due to the extreme nature of the stress. This happens when flight and fight are not options and the child goes into a third state called "freeze." In the freeze state, fear is overwhelming. The child perceives death as imminent and the result is massive permanent psychological and physiological changes in the mind-body complex.

As we saw in the last chapter, Pat and Angie have "parts" of them that exist inside the Limbic System. When I say "inside," I mean metaphorically. The wiring of the brain is in parallel, so many other structures—many that may be outside the actual Limbic System itself—are interconnected. But I want to use the analogy of "inside the box" to make a point. The fact is that during childhood development, the Limbic System *is* the brain that is in charge.

The brain forms sub-personalities to fulfill three basic functions: hold the pain, defend against the pain, and work to solve the problem of the pain. Angie has a part that carries the pain of shame. Her father was emotionally and physically unavailable to her. Her child brain assumed that he "didn't care" about her. This is almost certainly not true. More likely he was emotionally unable to show how much he really did care. Angie, the child, concluded that the problem was all about her. As the brain grows and develops, it takes what is learned and generalizes it. The generalization from this early learning would be an unconscious belief that "the world doesn't care about me."

Angie has another part, an angry part. This angry part is a protector of the hurt part. When she feels pain for even a millisecond, the angry part comes out to do battle by defending her against the pain. Meanwhile, Pat has a part that protects as well by making him avoid confrontation, so that the part of him that is afraid won't feel anxious anymore.

Conclusion

This brief chapter has covered a lot of ground, so let's summarize the concepts presented. We really have three distinct brains. The one that does all the important learning is the Limbic System, or the child's brain. Experience imprints it with beliefs, magical thinking, models of relationships, and many cognitive distortions based on strong emotions experienced when we are children. Dramatic learning from stress and abuse writes itself into the rapidly developing child-brain. Finally, at a late stage in the process, relationship learning occurs. This model of relationship, and any unmet emotional needs resulting from it, causes the still-coalescing brain to split into a system of sub-personalities or parts to deal with unwelcome pain.

The Limbic System is the automatic, self-preserving, instinctive brain that gives us a built-in template for how to operate in a relationship. The implication for adult relationships is serious. As humankind is evidently addicted to unconscious living and we teach our young the same, after the honeymoon is over couples turn the functioning of their relationship over to the child's brain, and become Lions and Unicorns battling it out from there.

Chapter 5

The Relationship between Perception, Feelings, and Behavior

Barbara Can't Find a Feeling

Barbara has spent the last fifteen minutes complaining about her husband. She does this every time she comes into my office. Evidently, he's quite a character. He constantly bullies her. Once or twice he has been a little physically violent. He regularly rages in front of their twin girls.

"I was going out of the house to come here this morning and he said, 'I suppose you're going to go fuck your therapist now.' Can you imagine? I don't understand how anyone could talk like that."

I look at her. I know she wants me to solve the problem. Her whole purpose in coming to therapy is for me to "solve the husband problem." In all the sessions we've had, she never once has asked me what any of this says about her. She's not concerned with her growth. She's only concerned with him. Therapy sessions begin and end with a litany of his abusive treatment and her indictment of him.

"In a few minutes the session will be over and you'll go home and see him. Thinking about that, how do you feel inside?"

"I feel like he's crazy. He'll probably scream at me some more. Why should anyone put up with that?"

"Barbara, why ask why? We know why he behaves like this. You told me that his parents died in an accident when he was three years old and he went through a series of foster homes. Remember that you told me how he was physically abused and ridiculed in that first home?"

"He's just so angry all the time. I can't handle his anger."

"Barbara, look at me." I'm hoping eye contact will help snap her out of the trance she's in. "I'm not excusing his behavior."

"You know what he tells me? He tells me that I think I'm perfect. He tells me that I think he's a piece of shit. I don't know how to deal with him."

I know I'm talking to a blank wall. Actually, I'm talking to a Unicorn whose defenses are so thick that she literally is not hearing a word I'm saying. Clearly, her husband is a Lion filled with shame from his early experiences. His "piece of shit" comment reveals the entire setup in the relationship. He thinks he's the "bad" one and she's the "good" one. He has enormous feelings of rejection driving his thoughts and behavior. This is Limbic Systems stuff.

She, as a Unicorn on the other hand, is living in mortal terror. She is counterbalancing his "badness" with her "goodness." She believes that if she remains calm and reasonable, he will eventually alter his behavior and things won't blow up. The problem is that she has no insight, because she's addicted to the drama of trying to be perfect to get him to settle down. What she doesn't realize is that her "perfection" keeps triggering his shame. Therefore, the very thing she's doing to solve the problem has become the problem from his point of view.

She's exasperated, "How am I expected to live like this? Why does he have to be so out of control? I try to keep the kids behaved. I clean the house. I cook his favorite food. Nothing seems to work. He's always so angry."

"Barbara, his behavior is out of your hands. The question is, 'What learning is available about you and what goes on inside of you?' For instance, when you see him about to get angry, what goes through your mind?"

"That there's no reason to get angry. Anger never solves anything. I just want to get away from him."

"What does anger mean to you, Barbara?"

"I don't know. What do you mean?"

"What feeling do you get when you think about anger?"

"That it's not right."

"Barbara, that's not a feeling. What emotion does your husband's anger trigger in you?"

"I just get frustrated."

I explain to Barbara that frustration is not a primary emotion. There has to be a feeling just underneath the frustration. She says, "I just feel like I'm walking on eggshells all the time."

"Great! What feeling is that, that walking on eggshells feeling?"

"I said, 'frustration.'" Now she's getting frustrated with me. But I'm undeterred.

"Barbara, I know this is difficult. If I told you I was walking on eggshells, how would you think I was feeling?"

She looks at me with a blank stare. "I don't know." What follows is nearly forty minutes of me trying to find various ways for her to get in touch with that "walking on eggshells" feeling. I use examples. I use metaphors. I cajole. I try bonding. Nothing is working. Why? Because my very questions are triggering the fear that she doesn't want to talk about or feel. I'm helpless. Don't get me wrong. This is all a pleasant exchange between us, but I would be better off talking about the Lakers.

Suddenly I have a great idea for a therapeutic intervention. This is one of those little exercises that I hope will turn on the light of insight. I ask her to stand in front of my big whiteboard and I hand her a marker. "Now, take the marker and let's write down some feelings or emotions. Go ahead."

The frustration leaves her for a moment as she sets to the task. "Okay," she mutters, "I need to write down the positive emotions first." With that, she jots "happy," "harmony," "joy," and "peace." She puts the marker down with a look of satisfaction.

As she does this, I nearly choke to death on my pride-filled anticipation. Trying to hold back my utter astonishment, I comment, "I'm wondering if you might include some negative emotions in the list."

She turns to the board and writes down "anger."

"Can you think of any others?"

"No, not really."

Mercifully, the hour is up.

Pat and Angie Discover the Feelings that Drive Behavior

As Pat and Angie file into the office, I'm still reeling from what just happened. I, unlike Barbara, am feeling all kinds of feelings. Did I push her too hard? How do I get her to wake up to what's going on inside of her? Wait a minute. *She* has to do that. I think that her next therapist will be the one that unlocks the door to her thoughts and feelings—I've failed. God, I hate listening to myself talk! Forty-five minutes of me being God's little helper and her just staring at me like I was from the planet Zulu. Were my questions as abusive as her husband's anger? If I were just a better therapist, if I was one of those passive, nice therapists with a big, open, vacant grin on my face she would like me more. My God! There's my issue of acceptance. Lord, forgive me for I have sinned. I have failed to become a better therapist three times since my last confession . . .

"Are you okay?" Angie asks me. I notice that she is looking at me intently as my misspent youth, Catholic guilt, and failed relationship with the Jesuits fade from my mind.

"Oh, no. I'm fine. Just mentally shifting gears." Yes, and I'm pumping myself up to believe I really am a good psychotherapist so I don't screw up this hour, too. I say to myself: Oh, man, there I go being hard on myself and beating myself up. Other therapists don't do that. Those really nice passive therapists never do any negative self-talk. I have to get my act together. My God. 'My act?' This can't be an act. I have to be real, handle my issues, and take care of my counter-transference—arrgh!

We exchange pleasantries while I slowly collect my thoughts. Suddenly I see Stewart Smalley from *Saturday Night Live* in my mind's eye there to help me, "You're good enough, and smart enough, and, by golly, people like you."

I try to conjure up my therapist smile to help me establish rapport. I just hope it doesn't reek of the superiority of someone who has been to graduate school and done personal growth work. "So, what have you noticed about yourselves and your relationship since we got together last?"

Pat is first out of the blocks. "I don't see what fear has to do with her anger."

I study him for a moment. There sounds like a bit of an edge to his tone. "You mean how does Angie's anger trigger fear in you?"

"Yeah, it seems like anger is anger. What else am I supposed to do but get away? Wouldn't anyone want to get away from anger?"

"You're probably right. Anyone would want to get away from anger. But let's look a little deeper. Are the two of you ready for a little thought experiment?"They both nod so I plunge ahead, sure of myself and what I'm doing once again. "Let's pretend that a large black dog just burst through the office door and is now racing around the room barking loudly. Pat, what would your first response be?"

Pat says, "What do you mean, my first response? You mean what do I want to do? I guess I would try to calm the dog down."

Angie looks at him a little wide-eyed. "That's not what I would do. I would look for the nearest way out of here."

"That's interesting, Angie. Why would you want to do that? What would your perception of the dog be?"

"That he would attack me, bite me. I don't like big dangerous dogs."

"Now, Angie, I'm going to ask Pat the same question. Pay very close attention to what he says. Pat, what is your perception of the dog that would prompt you to approach the dog?"

Pat thinks for a moment and then says, "Well, in my experience barking dogs are excited dogs, not dangerous dogs. So I would try to calm the dog down. Pet him, talk to him—that type of thing."

I address both of them. "Notice how fascinating this is. Presented with an identical circumstance, each of you perceives the situation dramatically differently."

Angie leans forward and gives her husband a curious look. "We do."

"What accounts for this difference in perception? And before you answer that, I want you to know that Pat has already answered the question."

"Experience," Pat interjects after a moment of silence. "My past experience is different than Angie's."

"Right. Do you see that, Angie?"

"Yes," she replies slowly.

"Given identical input into your five senses, the two of you would have dramatically different behaviors, in fact, opposite behaviors. So what's different?"

Angie suddenly gets a look of recognition in her eye, "Our perceptions are not the same."

"Right. So let's tie this into a simple model of behavior that will answer your original question, Pat," I say, gesturing to him. I go to the whiteboard and write out the following words:

Perception——————➤Feelings——————➤Behavior

Figure 5-1 The Internal Process

"Perception leads to feelings which lead to behavior. Now when we consider the barking dog example, Pat's perception was that the dog was excited. Pat, I'm guessing that led you to a feeling of confidence that you 'knew' what the dog was up to. Therefore, that generated the behavior of approaching the dog." I add those elements onto the board.

Excited   Confident   Approach
Perception——————➤Feelings——————➤Behavior

Figure 5-2 Dog Process A

"Now let's look at Angie's process surrounding the dog event. Her Perception was Danger. The Feeling was Fear. And the Behavior that she generated as a result was Withdrawal," I say as I write.

Excited   Confident   Approach
Perception——————➤Feelings——————➤Behavior
Danger   *Fear*   *Withdraw*

Figure 5-3 Dog Process A & B

At this point, I notice that I have the full attention of both of them. "Okay, Pat, now let's get to your original question about fear and anger. But let's put it into this cognitive model." I start erasing words, but I add a new one above the word "behavior."

Figure 5-4 The Internal Emotional Process

"Now, we know what the defensive behaviors are from our last session."
I briefly refer to the circles we drew on the board. "So let's fill that in."

Figure 5-5 Pat and Angie's defensive behavior

"Okay, Angie, what feeling is underneath your anger? Remember, last
week it was in the blue circle."

"He 'doesn't care' about me."

"Right, it's a shame feeling that he doesn't care. I'm going to change it
to read 'Nobody cares.'"

"And Pat. When you see Angie getting angry, what's that feeling you
feel?"

"Fear?"

"Yes, it's that 'Here we go again' feeling—a feeling of overwhelming
anxiety." Pat nods and I write it down.

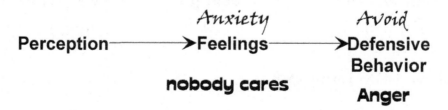

Figure 5-6 The feelings that drive the behavior

"Pat, what is your perception of what's happening or about to happen when you see her getting angry?"

"Things are going to get out of control . . ."

"Perfect," I cut in. "That's perfect."

"Angie, what's your perception when you get that 'He doesn't care about me' feeling?"

"I've been thinking a lot about this since our last session. Could it be that I feel he is rejecting me?"

"Absolutely! Man—you guys have it nailed today!"

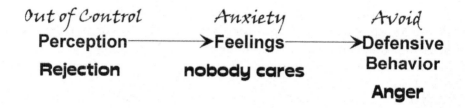

Figure 5-7 The perceptions that trigger the feelings

"Now, let me summarize. Angie, when it looks like you're being rejected, you feel that nobody cares about you and you get angry. And, Pat, when it looks like things are getting out of control, you feel anxious and you avoid and escape. You're out of there."

They nod vigorously. I pick up a marker and say, "Now watch what happens."

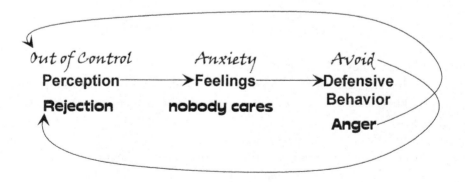

Figure 5-8 Interlocking, circular emotional processes

"Notice how one's defensive behavior triggers the other's distorted perception."

Pat wants to know what I mean by "distorted perception."

"Let's find out. Angie, when Pat avoids, what's your interpretation of his actions?"

"Just what it says. He's rejecting me. It seems pretty clear."

I turn to Pat and ask, "When you're avoiding Angie, what are you really trying to do?"

He has a note of exasperation in his voice as he replies, "I'm trying to get her to calm down. I just want some peace."

I turn to the board and erase the lines and arrows. I write as I talk. "So, Pat wants peace. That's his hoped-for outcome, or the goal of his defensive behavior. Now, Pat, what's your interpretation of Angie's anger?"

"She's trying to push me away."

"Angie, is that true?"

Her face turns red and she hollers, "No, it's not true! I want him to come closer."

I write more on the board, which now looks like this:

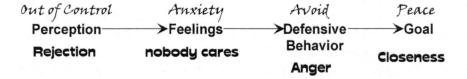

Figure 5-9 Insane strategies

"By the way," I comment in an off-handed manner, "we have just defined insanity."

"What?" they ask nearly in unison.

I chuckle, "Of course. No one who thinks avoidance brings peace is thinking clearly. And for sure anger is not a breeding ground for closeness."

Fortunately, Pat and Angie are not offended.

"Look," I say. "The point is that you are both persistently doing what doesn't work. Your Limbic System, the child brain, thinks that avoidance creates peace and anger brings another closer. But the three of us adults sitting here obviously know better."

Angie looks at me with sudden recognition in her eyes. "Boy, I better work on my anger."

Pat says, "You mean I need to stay and listen to her yell at me?" A look of horror sweeps over his face.

"No, I'm not suggesting that. Let's go back to our earlier diagram, because I skipped over something I want to discuss. Can I erase some of this?"

"No!" Angie asks for a piece of paper and copies down the diagram. When she is finished, she looks up at me and says, "Okay, now you can erase it."

I set to work and the drawing reverts to this earlier version:

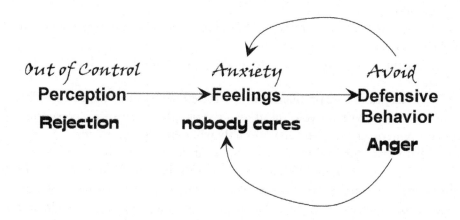

Figure 5-10 Defensive behavior is an emotional defense against feelings we don't want to feel.

Then I add a couple of large arrows. "Remember we used the term 'defensive behavior.' That means the behavior is a defense against something. If we look at the diagram, the cognitive process clearly tells us that the purpose of the defense is to defend against the feeling. Why are we defending against the feeling? Because we don't want to feel the feeling."

Angie has a sudden expression of recognition. "You mean that my anger is so I don't feel like 'nobody cares'?"

"Right. That 'nobody cares' feeling is a bad feeling. In fact, the feeling is always as big as the defense we use. For you, Angie, that means your anger is as big as the pain that's underneath the anger."

"And my need to avoid is as big as my fear?"

"That's right, Pat. The more you want to get away, the bigger the feeling from which you're getting away. In other words, you're not avoiding Angie. You're escaping your own feelings of overwhelm, anxiety, nervousness, and pressure. It's a survival tactic that you learned as a child."

We go over this for a few minutes. Finally, the question that is clearly on the table is: "How do we change our behavior?"

"It's natural that you would ask that question. When clients get their first glimpse of what's really going on inside of them, that's the first question they ask." I gesture back to the board. "Remember, this is an automatic, self-preserving, emotional process that is embedded in neural nets deep inside the brain. We can't just go to the end of the process and force ourselves to change."

Angie looks at me and asks, "Shouldn't I go take anger management classes to get rid of my anger?"

"Again, that would seem to make sense. But look what's on the board."

"Perception. The problem is my distorted perception, like you said."

"Exactly. What you need—and you, too, Pat—is 'perception management' classes. And that's exactly what we're going to do."

Pat moves forward in his seat. "So what do we do in the meantime?"

"Ah, great question. What I want you to do is to become experts in noticing your defenses. In other words, Pat, I want you to become an expert on your need to avoid. Watch yourself avoid, become the avoidance detective." I explain to them that they will not be able to do this in real time at first. It will occur to them the next day or even days later that they had been defensive. But gradually they will be able to watch themselves become defensive as it's happening.

"The real goal is to feel the feeling that you do not want to feel. But first we need to study our defensive process, and become mindful of how we do it."

Pat and Angie leave, not totally convinced. I know from experience that it will take several more sessions before they can "get with the program."

Chapter 6

The Internal Process

The concept that perception leads to feelings, which leads to defensive behavior, seems simple enough. But underlying it is a deep process that goes on in many circumstances throughout the day. This disturbing fact flies in the face of what motivates people to go to counseling. After all, aren't we looking for the problem that occurs only during those big emotional explosions in life? Isn't the root of a married couple's trouble the "thing" that happens when they fight? Shouldn't we be looking for that issue that keeps us stuck, so we can get unstuck? Actually, the answer is no.

What we're looking for is something so big that it presents itself in even the most mundane events throughout the day. In other words, the "problem" we're trying to "solve" is huge, all-encompassing, and has been hanging out in the Limbic System since we were four, five, or six years old. Sure, it may *look* like it's associated with our marriage, our dead-end career, or our bad habits—but that's a misapprehension. The misapprehension is that we have a problem only when life is not working. And we only notice that life is not working when it blows up in our face.

I liken it to the alcoholic family. In AA parlance, the alcohol is the "elephant" that no one wants to acknowledge or talk about. Imagine a family sitting around the living room with an elephant, each family member in his or her own way pretending that the ponderous pachyderm is not there. The only time they acknowledge its presence is when the alcoholic acts out. If we study alcoholism and the family, we find that each family member has their own agenda for leaving the elephant unacknowledged.

To a tragic extent, Lions and Unicorns (all of us) are doing the same thing. When someone walks into my office, he or she is dragging this large unacknowledged "thing." I can usually see it in a few minutes. It may take them many months to see it. Some may never see it. How can that be? How can they ignore something so large? If I see it so clearly, why can't they?

The answer is simple: conditioning. This "thing" has been with us since we were very young. We are so well adjusted to its always being there that we don't notice it anymore. We've built up ways of thinking, perceiving, and feeling that are so automatic that the only thing we notice is the defense we've developed to keep ourselves from seeing it. And this defense seems to us to be so natural, reasonable, and obvious that we never question it. It has become second nature.

Let's explore three elements of the "thing," starting from the end of the process and working toward the beginning. By the time we get back to the starting place of the process, we'll be able to see the problem for what it really is: (1) We have held a worldview in our heads since the beginning of our social lives. (2) Then there is the pain of unmet emotional needs that we carry silently. And (3) there are our efforts to simply protect ourselves from a threatening and hostile world.

Defensive Behavior

Defensive behavior is at the back end of the process we are analyzing. To get at it, let's first define what a defense is.

Freud was the first to document so-called psychological defenses. He enumerated them, and good students of psychology at some point must memorize them. The first among them is denial, followed by avoidance and repression. The list ends with something called sublimation, which means that you play golf or do pottery when you really are horny.

For our present purpose, we'll talk about only two defenses: anger and avoidance. Anger is easy to spot. There are mild forms of anger when a person just has a look or a slight tone in their voice. Yelling, raising of voices, frustration, even jealousy are all forms of anger. Whining and complaining is anger. These forms of anger are important since trying to put a mask on anger won't hide it. Someone who is *scanning* for anger will pick it up immediately. This is important to understand since even masked anger can trigger the defenses of a person whose survival strategies depend heavily on detecting it.

Avoidance is a little more complex. On the surface, it would seem that avoidance is simple. Someone who is avoiding is not available. But what does that mean? A person who avoids might simply walk away. They get up and go hide. In this case, avoidance has elements of escape—I'm outahere!

Not responding, stony silence, cutting someone off emotionally—these are all avoidance. A person does this in many ways. Pretending, placating, or even promising are various ways of making oneself emotionally unavailable. Laying low is avoidance.

The Purpose behind a Defense

"Defense" is the word used for a simple reason: Being angry or avoidant is a defense against something. When we defend, we're attempting to protect ourselves from some real or perceived threat or problem. What is weird about defending is that we think a defense is supposed to change the outcome somehow. So our defending has a kind of warped goal, in that we think our defending behavior will alter the other person's behavior. If this really worked, defending wouldn't be called defending. We would call it changing, transforming, or negotiating. The idea that a defense can achieve an outcome other than sheer protection is a folly of human nature.

What, then, is a defense supposed to do? Alter our feelings. If we can attack, blame, avoid, ignore, or in some way minimize the other person, we get to feel better.

As human beings, we have yet to learn that we are 100 percent responsible for our own feelings and emotions. In our child's mind, if we can lay responsibility at the feet of someone else, we can then justify a full-scale attack on him or her. After all, if it weren't for that person, I wouldn't feel the way I do.

To put it simply, we use an emotional, psychological defense for one purpose and one purpose only: to make a feeling go away. I had a client once who was going through the process of refinancing his home. The qualification process was embarrassing to him and he noticed himself beginning to get angry. As he did, he also noticed the embarrassment go away. Bingo! The light went on in his head. He clearly saw how his use of anger made him feel better.

Avoidance is no different from anger in terms of its use as a defense. The purpose behind avoiding is not to get away from the other person, but to make a feeling go away. If we notice someone avoiding or using anger, we should note that that person is in the process of trying to feel better.

The Physiological Cost

Hmmm, let's see. I've spent most of my adult life trying to feel better by producing a behavior to alter my feeling state. If I'm honest about it, I admit that I use this defense many times a day to make myself feel better. Wait a minute! This sounds a lot like substance abuse. Every time I need to feel better, I take a hit of strong chemicals and hormones to alter my physiological state—to feel better. Could it be that I'm chemically addicted to my psychological defense?

Anger certainly releases many substances into the brain and bloodstream. So does avoidance. We're suddenly back to the flight or fight syndrome. It doesn't just stop there, however. There is another substance that's released during our defensive responses that helps keep us trapped in them: endorphins, the brain's "feel good chemical." Our defense is a result of a perceived stressor, a threat. The stress response in the brain releases endorphins that in a real-life-threatening situation serve to blunt the effects of pain.

There is a very real implication to the release of endorphins as we act out our psychological defenses. First, the defense is a learned response. Cognitive theory and our own experience both tell us that a process involving thinking and feeling precedes even the most conditioned automatic behavior. The question becomes, then, how is it that the brain thinks that my wife's nagging or my husband's failure to acknowledge me is a life-threatening situation? After all, aren't we adults now?

Unfortunately, we're not adults. We're children, or at least we were children when this defense imprinted itself on the Limbic System. Flight or fight is the brain's response to stress—a perceived threat. As a result, the response is massive. The physiological consequences are large and multifarious. Perhaps most importantly, our defenses are a child's response to a threat on his or her life. The child who first learns to flee or fight is fighting or fleeing for survival, quite literally.

The logical conclusion is that the child who learns flight or fight— avoidance or anger—is trying to stay alive. Whatever it was that happened in those formative years was perceived by the child as life-threatening. The adult who calls this response into play repeatedly has long since learned to survive and is now merely addicted to the habit. We become defense junkies. And like the drug addict or alcoholic we have our excuses, our philosophy, our story—we have become addicted to the drama of it all. We're unconscious, reactive automatons run by a primitive part of the brain that thinks it's saving our lives with each encounter.

Passive vs. Active

The picture we have here is not pretty. Lions and Unicorns are chasing each other's tails while pretending to be grown-up humanoids. There is a qualitative difference between their two styles of defense, however. Lions, using anger, have what I call an active defense. It is "in-your-face," in everybody's face. Anger is hard to ignore or escape. It's hard to be with an angry person even when the anger is not directed at you.

Avoidance, on the other hand, is passive. Escaping, getting away, not responding, a lack of reaction, these are all passive behaviors that can be hard to spot. Avoidance is more socially acceptable than anger. For this reason, it is a temptation to label the Lion "the bad one" and the Unicorn "the good one" in a relationship. More often than not, trained therapists make this unwarranted and unwise value judgment, which is not helpful to successfully healing a relationship.

The problem is that most therapists, psychologists, and psychiatrists are Unicorns. These professions attract passively defended people, who in turn reinforce the cultural stereotypes right in the psychotherapy room.

This passive act on the part of the Unicorn doesn't fool me, though. These people are often angry and resentful, with just as much to work on as their Lion counterparts do. More often than not, I will point this out, then turn to the Lion and tell them that their acting-out anger is giving the Unicorn cover. The illusion is that as long as the Lion keeps getting angry there is no reason for the Unicorn to work on their own issues. Often the Unicorn will sit passively with a smug look while the Lion rages about not getting the approval they want in the relationship. I have to bust the Unicorn's cover. This isn't easy, as most Unicorns want you to believe that they're "good, reasonable" people.

Lions are not slick at expressing their feelings. They are out front. Unicorns are slick, covert—so good at being passively angry that they have convinced themselves that they have no hidden agenda. Getting Unicorns to see how they are punishing their partner is not easy. Neither is getting Lions to forget their guilt and do the work of learning awareness.

Feelings

Next let's look into feelings, the middle element of the cognitive process that has defensive behavior at its result, and distorted perception as its trigger.

Feelings or emotions drive behavior. Bad emotions drive defensive behavior. "Bad" emotions are feelings we don't want to feel. They're emotions we *never* want to feel. I call them "exiled" feelings. These feelings are so big and bad that we spend our entire lives trying not to feel them. We organize our world around not feeling them. These young, childlike, vulnerable parts of us carry overwhelming despair and pain.

We all carry a wounded child-self inside of us. Where do these wounds come from? Children need people who can mirror back to them a sense of their own preciousness. We need to see ourselves reflected back in our mother's and father's eyes with love and compassion and acceptance. A parent's own sense of woundedness, however, restricts his or her ability to extend themselves authentically to their child.

Parents who don't want to see their own pain steadfastly deny the pain of their children. Too often, in varying degrees, we avoid our own pain by emphasizing the child's deficiencies. This can come in the form of indirect criticism, outright verbal assault, or the tragedy of abuse. We raise generation after generation of children in households marked by alcoholism, drug abuse, violence, rage, and emotional manipulation.

Often clients tell me that their parents "did the best they could." I ask how they did their best. Did they read a book on how to raise children? Did they attend a parenting class? More often than not, parenting is the random process of repeating the patterns handed down from one generation to the next. This is not enlightened child-rearing. This is inertia. Being well-intentioned doesn't mean doing your best.

We all experience conditional love. Conditional love says that a child must meet certain expectations, hide certain parts of themselves that are unacceptable, and definitely never show weaknesses, fears, or pain. I do not want to see my child's pain. To empathize with the child, I must know about my own pain. I've been on the run from that all my life!

Conditional love conditions the mind, the Limbic System—specifically the flight or fight response. The conditioned mind of the terrified, angry child runs the brain of the adult. It is the source of all of the sorrow of humankind.

The Needs of the Lion and Unicorn

This exiled pain we carry from childhood, this sense of woundedness comes from the experience of not getting what we needed from our earliest meaningful relationship. For Lions and Unicorns, these are two dramatically different needs.

Erik Erikson assumed that all children go through stages of development sequentially in sort of a stair-step fashion. The first two stages are trust vs. mistrust and autonomy vs. shame. My view is that early attachment is this "trust vs. mistrust" stage. This forms the child's original orientation to the world. Security needs are driven by attachment instincts operating from deep inside the brain. This all happens nonverbally mediated by the right orbital frontal cortex in close connection to the Limbic System. The third stage of development is social development. Here I believe that the last two Eriksonian stages (initiative vs. guilt, and industry vs. inferiority) take place simultaneously.

To see into the core of the Lion-Unicorn dynamic, we need to focus on the first two stages. While issues of trust and autonomy are important to all children, trust is paramount in the mind of the Unicorn and autonomy is paramount in the mind of the Lion. Let me put it more simply and in language that is more emotional. Unicorns care about one thing primarily—*safety*. Lions care about one thing primarily—*approval*. The residual result of safety issues are mistrust or fear. The residual of approval issues is shame.

This observation fits neatly with my earlier discussion of temperament. On one hand, the mild, cautious child will naturally be interested in a world that is not chaotic, out of control, overly hostile and threatening, or too risky. On the other hand, the bolder child is interested in a world that rewards daring, adventure, and skill—that puts a premium on recognition, acceptance, and encouragement.

Lions want to know that their more aggressive nature is acceptable. When a cat catches a mouse, you are to watch the cat play with the trophy. The Lion wants the reward of approval. Because of this, they take everything personally.

Unicorns don't take things personally. They don't want the spotlight. They are content to be in the background. They just want space to do it their way in their own time.

The unmet emotional need for approval in the child-lion results in shame, just as Erikson predicts. Similarly, the unmet emotional need for safety produces mistrust or fear in the child-unicorn.

Therefore, the woundedness that the Lion carries into a relationship is a feeling of shame—not being good enough, feeling rejected, unacceptable, unloved, unappreciated, unfit for human contact, disrespected, unimportant, and disregarded. I did not invent these words to write a book. These are the actual exiled feelings expressed in session after session in my office by Lions working on relationships.

The woundedness of the Unicorn is far different. It is fear, anxiety, a sense of overwhelm, a feeling of walking on eggshells, nervousness. This happens on three levels that I have noticed:

1. The "fear-of-failure level" is the "Whatever I do will not work" level. The Unicorn thinks, "If I do *this*, it won't make them happy. If I do *that*, it won't make them happy. This feels very uncomfortable. I better not do anything." The feeling of discomfort results in paralysis.

2. The next level of fear is the fear of conflict. To a Unicorn, everything looks like it will lead to conflict. Potential conflict is everywhere. To a Unicorn, any emotional energy is potential conflict. I can't predict which one of these fears, fear of failure or fear of conflict, will predominate. In my experience, fear of conflict is more prevalent.

3. Underlying both of these fears is a third fear. The fear of rejection is the bottom line for Unicorns. They desperately want the closeness of a safe relationship, but the cost is loss of space, freedom, and breathable air. That's right. Unicorns feel they will be smothered. The formal term for this is fear of engulfment. What this does is set up a desperate push-pull dynamic, the need for closeness offset by the need for freedom.

Perception

Perception is at the front end of the defensive behavior. It's where the "thing" starts. It's also the single most difficult concept to explain. The concept itself isn't that difficult. But we are so addicted to our own habitual way of looking at things that it never occurs to us, until someone points it out in a rare moment when we might actually hear them, that there are other versions of reality.

The biochemistry driving the habitual viewpoint is almost mechanical. The Amygdala, as outlined earlier, first processes incoming information for emotional content. The Hippocampus then takes that information and searches memory. Unless the cortex subsequently questions what the

Limbic Systems dishes up from the bowels of the brain, we take what we get from that neurological process as unquestionable and unchallengeable.

It may be true that the traits we see in others are actually there. Objects, events, behaviors, and behavioral patterns may in fact be really there in front of us. All of these things travel from the outside-in to the Thalamus—except for smell, which travels directly to the Amygdala.

The meaning we assign to what is happening, however, does not travel from outside in. It travels from inside out. In brief, we make it up. Perception is a function of combining mental associations in the Limbic System with previously processed emotions. The form, in and of itself, carries no emotion with it. The emotional content is something the Limbic System adds so that we know whether to flee or fight.

Therefore, meaning or perception is a function of our brains, not something determined by the other person. All of the emotional pain we experience in a relationship is a function of our internal process of creating perceptions.

This is so clear logically, and yet so difficult for people to accept. We desperately want someone else to blame. Taking responsibility for our own emotional reactions and our perception of the behavior in others is the first and hardest step for anyone to take. But it is true that our partner does not have the power to make us feel anything. What we choose to feel is entirely a function of our own internal process.

Perception is a function of the meaning we are projecting onto others all of the time. Tragically, this means that we never see reality for what it is. We live in a prison dictated by the meaning our primitive brain is casting over the people and events around us.

Perception is the first stage in the life-preserving, automatic process of the Lion and the Unicorn. This process never fundamentally changes. The pain is the pain—either fear or shame. The reaction is always the same. The behavior can be a little different from time to time. Our perception can modulate it. But it nearly always boils down to either anger or avoidance.

In later chapters, we will explore important variations on these behaviors. Fundamentally, however, we need to understand the internal process we carry inside of us. For Lions, perception triggers shame which prompts anger. For Unicorns, perception triggers fear which prompts avoiding. Events, real or imagined, trigger this process repeatedly throughout the day. It's a prison. We're its slaves. Yet, we feel totally justified in our point of view, our rationalization. The dance continues.

Chapter 7

The Unconscious Stuff of Internal Process

Lisa Disowns Her Weakness and Vulnerability

Lisa has arrived for her first appointment. She is a striking dark-haired woman of about 35, wearing a tight-fitting business suit. She is the branch manager of a local independent bank. One of the first things she asks is if I know about families that adopt children. I say yes and inquire as to why that's important. She says that her husband adopted a nephew long before they were married, and the relationship between her husband and the nephew is the source of the problem.

"Why is that a problem?" I ask.

"It's just the way my husband treats him. He coddles him and fusses over him. My God, the kid is 13. He'll never grow up to be a man."

"How is that a problem for you?"

"My husband wants me to treat his nephew that way, too. I can't do it. It's not right."

Right away, the problem becomes apparent. I don't need to know whether or not her husband is really coddling the boy. He may be or not, it really doesn't matter. What matters is that Lisa's perception is that the boy is being coddled. This means that when she "sees" that, something happens inside of her. Her objection to the way her husband deals with the boy tells me everything I need to know about her. It tells me nothing about the husband or the boy.

"I'm just curious, what's your reaction when you see this interaction?"

"Oh, I get angry. I don't want to be around them. My husband thinks I'm rejecting the boy, that I don't care about him. It's not that at all. I just would prefer to do my own thing. Plus, I don't want to watch them anymore. It drives me crazy."

So far, Lisa has revealed a lot about herself. When she sees her husband and his adoptive son interact, she sees something she doesn't want to see. That perception brings up a feeling that she doesn't want to feel. She then defends against that feeling with anger. The key to understanding this process is that what triggers all of this is something she doesn't want to see in herself. She has a huge objection to this thing inside of her, and must defend against it at all costs.

I noticed something else. She said she likes to "do her own thing." This indicates a lifestyle choice, a way of being in the world. I wonder if she'll confirm this with embedded comments as we go along.

"Let me get just a little background from you, okay?" Over the course of the rest of the hour, her story unfolds. She is the youngest of five children. All of her siblings were boys and she was the baby in the family. Mom and Dad worked hard from the time that Lisa was young enough to be in daycare. Much of the "care" she received came from her brothers, who looked after her responsibly, but were four older boys.

During the course of the conversation, Lisa repeats a theme in her own language that I know is hidden from her, but all too blatant to me. Mom taught her to "be independent." The family issued emotional rewards when someone "showed initiative" or "didn't need help" or "did it themselves." The family injunction was clear: "Be strong, and don't be weak." And to Lisa the injunction went further: "Don't be the weak *girl*, and don't be a *baby*." In other words, at some level she must have felt that in order to survive she needed to deny who she was in the family.

How rich it is, then, that she has married into a situation that constantly brings up her objection to her own vulnerability!. Every time she sees her husband coddle his son, she projects herself into the son and thinks, oh no, that's weakness and vulnerability. That can't be revealed. I must defend. And she continues to show only strength, confidence, and competence in her relations with others.

To help her, I must be like Captain Kirk. I must take her "where no one has gone before" —right into the vulnerability she is trying so hard to avoid. It may not be easy. She is convinced, as we end the session, that this problem is all about her husband and not about her. And it may well be that her husband has a disabling parenting style. He may indeed have some issue that compels him to be a rescuer. He did, after all, adopt the boy and now treats him like a victim. But none of that is important until Lisa sees what *she* is doing. She can't use the force of her will to change him, she can only change herself.

The Root of Pat's Problem with Anger

Pat is right out of the blocks as our session begins. "I'm having a real problem with this anger thing."

"What's that Pat?"

"Well, it seems like you're saying that it's okay for someone to be angry. I just don't understand that. Anger is never okay. It never accomplishes anything. It's a waste of time."

Pat looks edgy and I don't want to confront that. I need to validate what he's saying. I want him to understand that I'm on his side, and I need to that without *taking* sides. "Being in the presence of anger makes me uncomfortable, too, Pat. Do you think Angie knows how big her anger really is sometimes?"

"I'm sure she doesn't. But just as a basic philosophy, anger just isn't okay. Why can't some people understand that?"

Angie is looking at Pat as if he's crazy. "I have a right to be angry! Plus, he's plenty angry himself."

"I only get angry when you're in my face, bitching at me."

I step in immediately. I never sit back in a session and let acting-out get out of hand. "Okay, let's not go there."

They sit back and settle down. I let a moment pass before I continue. "Pat, I think I hear you saying that you have a huge objection to anger. You need to understand that this is not a philosophy. It is an emotional reaction. Feelings drive all behavior. That includes our philosophy, our point of view, and our need to be right."

Pat mumbles something and I say, "Pat, right there—what are you doing? You're being defensive. I'm making no value judgment. Just notice what you're doing. You're angry. In fact, you're just as angry as Angie is."

He sits up and looks at me. "I am?"

"Of course. You just don't express your anger. It's the expression of anger, the acting out of anger that you object to. Make no mistake about it, you are plenty angry. The problem here is that you have a huge objection to your anger."

"I hate anger," he admits.

"That is a Unicorn trait. Unicorns hate anger and they will avoid expressing anger at all costs unless they feel cornered or trapped. Then they will fight like mad. So what they do instead is find a variety of passive ways to express their aggression. They show up late, they don't call, they break promises. Unicorns are the covert sneak attackers in the relationship. The problem for the Lions is that they never see it coming. These jungle tactics keep the Lion in a constant state of uproar. And inevitably what happens is that the Lion gets to act out all of the anger in the relationship."

As I say this, I see Angie's eyes literally bug out. "I always wondered why I was so angry."

"In effect, Pat, by refusing to express your anger honestly, you are goading her into expressing it."

"She's good at it, all right."

That was an attack and I decide to confront it head on. "Pat, I'm sure that makes you feel like you're better than her. As she becomes more and more crazy in the relationship, you must get a smug satisfaction. You're setting her up. Trust me. none of this makes you look good either."

A look of realization is sweeping over Angie's face. "Oh my God! I never saw it before. I just kept taking the bait, didn't I?"

I smile at her and say, "Oh, yeah. It was just like waving sirloin in front of a hungry cat. You took the bait every time."

I turn back to Pat. "You see, being passively angry is still being angry. The real issue is what feeling the anger stirs up inside of you. When you notice Angie getting angry, what feeling comes up inside of you?"

Pat still looks a little shell-shocked at my having blown his cover. "I just want to get away."

"Right, but that's the defensive behavior. What is the feeling that is inside of you when that happens?"

"I feel pressure. It's uncomfortable."

"I understand. Is that the same thing as anxiety?"

"Yes." Pat now has the ability to feel the feeling instead of numbing out or shutting down the feeling. It's more accessible to him.

"But what happens to the anger, Pat?"

"I don't know. I guess I don't feel it."

"Right. Where do you think it goes?"

"I don't know. I don't think I'm angry."

"Thinking back to your father for a few minutes, what were some of the things he did that really upset you?"

Pat thinks for a moment. I can tell he is visually remembering scenes with his father because he is looking up and to the left with his eyes.

I let Pat process through what he's seeing for a moment. Noticing his eye movement reminds me of Neuro-Linguistic Programming™ (NLP™). When we look up to the left, we are visually recalling something. When we look up to the right, we are imagining something for the first time. Oftentimes, imagining will require constructing an image: Usually people will stare straight ahead and defocus their eyes when they are doing that. They are literally building visualization in the space in front of them. Most people recall sounds by literally looking toward their left ear. A person looking toward the right ear is making up a sound or listening to a sound not heard before.

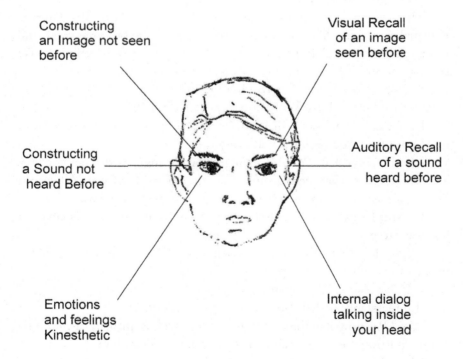

Figure 7-1 NLP Eye Accessing Cues

We often have internal dialogs. It's easy to determine when someone is internally talking to themselves because they look down and to the left. Looking down and to the right is a sure sign of someone checking out his or her feelings.

"Pat, I notice you are looking up here." I gesture in the general direction to which he keeps looking. "Often when we remember a picture, we position it in a certain spot in space. Is that about the spot?"

Pat nods and looks at me a bit quizzically.

"Don't lose the internal picture. Describe it to me."

"I see my Dad beating me."

"That must be a difficult picture to see. Is the picture big or little?"

"Oh, it's a big picture."

"Is it dim or bright?" I ask.

"It's dark."

"Okay, is it in color or black and white?"

"Color."

"How about movement? Is it like a movie or a still picture?"

"It's a movie. I can see him hitting me."

Pat has a look of distress on his face. "What feeling do you feel inside your body as you look at the picture? Any emotion at all?"

Pat hold his hand to his stomach and says, "Fear, I'm scared he's going to hit me."

"What is he doing in the picture?"

"He's yelling at me, threatening me."

I tell Pat to allow his mind to let go of the picture for a few minutes while we talk about something else. I ask him to point with his index finger to a picture that's on the wall across the room. I instruct him to cover first one eye and then the other.

"Do you notice how your finger jumps back and forth as you do that?"

"Yeah, I do."

"Take your time and do it again. Tell me which one of your eyes is actually looking at the end of your finger and on to the picture?"

"My right eye."

"The reason for the little exercise is to establish which eye is your dominant eye. You can do the same thing when you stand over a golf ball. You will find that we tend to use one eye consistently to target our vision."

Pat smiles at me. "Okay, Doc, what's the point?"

"It must seem pretty strange for me to jump from this dramatic experience with your father to some weird deal with your eye. But it turns out that you have two internal eyes too."

Pat looks at me as if I have just lost it for real.

"Pat," I laugh, "I'm trying to have a dramatic moment here. Just bear with me and this will make some sense. I promise." I take a breath in preparation for trying to explain what I want him to do next.

"Just as we have two external eyes, we have two internal eyes. This is because we have two hemispheres in our brain—right and left." I gesture up and to Pat's right. "Go back to that picture of your father for a moment. As you look at that internal picture, allow yourself to become aware of which internal eye you are using to look at that picture. This will feel like the internal image is linked to an external eye."

Pat takes a moment and says, "Right."

"Good, that's great. Now, while you're looking at that picture with your right internal eye, allow your mind to let you become aware of what you're seeing with your left internal eye. You will have a feeling that this image is connected to the non-dominate external eye."

This is a bit of a gamble since I never know what a person might see out of their non-dominant internal eye. But this exercise is so powerful and revealing that it almost always provides a doorway into an area that the client has never explored.

A pioneering NLP practitioner named Allen Sargent was researching visualization and hemispheric dominance when he discovered that we have two "mind's eyes," one associated with each hemisphere. Incredible! Since the left eye connects to the right hemisphere, the left internal eye connects to the right hemisphere. Of course, the reverse is true for the other eye. What makes this powerful is that the right hemisphere has to do with our emotional selves and expresses itself nonverbally. It speaks to us in metaphors and emotional memories. Some say that the right hemisphere is the subconscious mind. I prefer to think of this information as simply out of our awareness.

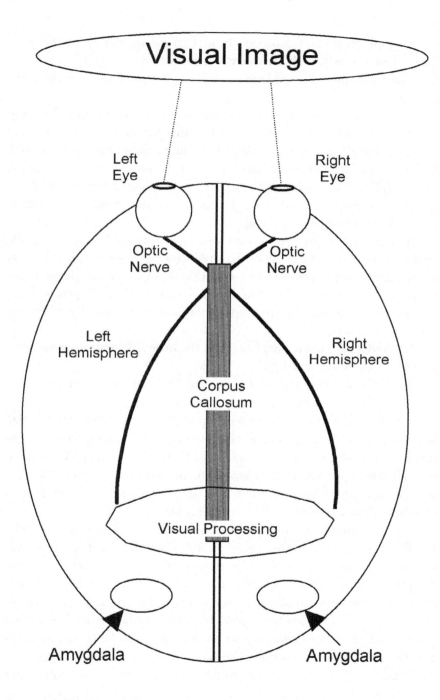

Figure 7-2 The Visual Crossover

Pat looks at me and shakes his head. I encourage him, "Just take your time. There is a picture there. You're just not used to seeing it."

After a moment he suddenly says, "I see a cage. I'm in a cage. I feel trapped."

I ask Pat the same series of questions as before regarding the description of the picture. It turns out that this picture is further away and off to the left a little. It is also black and white and not very well focused. In NLP™ parlance, these various aspects of the internal image are called sub-modalities. A modality is the way we code something in terms of our senses. A bright sunny day is bright because of our visual acuity. Vision then is the modality we are using.

Sub-modalities are the sensory aspects of internal images. We code images according to the qualities they have and the way we represent them to ourselves. Sound, color, brightness, feelings and various other sensory textures alter our experience of internal images. NLP™ practitioners use sub-modalities to alter the representational image and therefore our reactions and beliefs.

". . . and, Pat, what feeling goes with the image? Feel inside your body. Can you sense a feeling there?"

Pat takes a moment. I can tell he's still "looking" at the caged image. "I'm mad. I'm mad that he has me trapped."

I instruct Pat to move the image up so that it becomes equal in size and distance to the image in his other internal eye. Then I instruct him to move both images a little closer and make them a little larger. We work on making the trapped image as clear as the other image. I'll have Pat alter these images later. First I want him to be able to access his feelings. He has shut himself down emotionally most of his life..

Shutting down emotionally is common to the Unicorn type. The thinking is that if the Unicorn pretends he or she feels no feelings, there will be no exterior reaction for the parent to see. If the parent sees no reaction, then they will presumably go away, thereby leaving the Unicorn in peace. In essence, the Unicorn acts like they sever all the nerves to their face in an effort to stay emotionally invisible. It's a lot like playing dead or playing possum. The problem is that the act becomes a reality. Once ensconced in a relationship they are emotionally dead, unavailable—nobody home.

"Pat, the objective is for you to feel your feelings—to be fully aware of them and let them guide you in making decisions. If you are acting out passively, without being aware, the bottom line is that you could be punishing Angie for something she didn't do. In reality, you're punishing your father for something he *did* do, and your child brain doesn't know the difference. With full access to your feelings, your adult brain can use awareness to make decisions. One of those choices might be to tell Angie when you're feeling angry so she might have a chance to know when she has crossed one of your boundaries."

"Yes, but I don't want to be angry."

I look at Pat with empathy. "I know. The angry part of you is a part that you've disowned. Would it ever have been safe for you to show your father how angry you were?"

Pat shakes his head and I continue. "Since expressing anger was something that was never allowed and not safe, it had to go underground. The simple fact is that, as an adult, you have every right to experience and to express anger. It is never okay to act out anger."

Angie, who has been silent for some time, finally pipes up. "You keep saying 'express anger but don't act out anger.' I don't know the difference."

"Expressing anger is easy. When I feel anger, I say 'I'm angry.' When I act out anger, I shout and scream 'I'm angry!' Interestingly, expressing a feeling is far more powerful and effective than acting it out."

Chapter 8

Sub-Personalities

In chapter four, I stated that the brain forms sub-personalities to fulfill three basic functions: hold the pain; defend against the pain, and work to solve the problem of the pain. This chapter explores in a little more detail how that happens.

The developing Limbic System, along with the early parts of the Cortex to which it is wired, develops sub-personalities—or *parts*—to cope with the life situations into which we are thrust as children. "Why does this happen?" one might ask. The reason is developmental. Until around age five, we just don't have sufficient wiring in the prefrontal Cortex to reason through the vagaries of a relationship.

It would be nice if a youngster could think, "Now, I know Mom is not giving me a reflection of my own preciousness because she was deeply hurt and made wary by a dysfunction in her relationship with her father, so I shouldn't take her alcoholism personally." But a child simply doesn't have the brainpower to think this way.

This situation was brought home to me recently when one of my clients reported talking to his children about his anger. He told them that he is recognizing that his anger has been a bit out of control and that he needs to change. He was checking in with them to see if they had felt the effects of too much anger. His four-year-old son piped up and said, "Daddy, you get too mad."

He smiled and said that he is going to try very hard not to be so angry. His son responded in kind by saying, "And I won't be so bad."

What this tragically illustrates is that the mind of a child cannot conceive of a hero-parent being fatally flawed. As children we assume, with lifelong consequences, that the fault is ours. This little boy had assumed that Daddy's anger was a function of his bad behavior.

At some point after the attachment phase, the child picks "the relationship" into which he or she will enter as a unique and separate individual. This is significantly different than the bonding that occurs with the mother during the first three years. Attachment has the purpose of the organism's survival. A relationship has the purpose of belonging to this world in a safe and satisfying way, as a child tries to join the outside world. To learn how to do this, the child must try it out on someone. Each of us picks one or the other of our parents, if that's who raised us, for this role.

If things don't go well in this first social encounter, the child, as a result, must cope with the painful emotions surrounding its first effort to engage in social intercourse. The child's primitive brain compartmentalizes this pain and its consequences by forming sub-personalities or parts.

The development of these parts initially follows the progression we have seen in our cognitive model:

Perception ➤ Feelings ➤ Defensive Behavior

Figure 8-1 The Cognitive Process

The Part That Carries the Pain

How do we even get emotional pain? Not everyone has horrible childhood experiences. Not all of us get beaten about the head and shoulders by a drunken step-father every Saturday night for years, although many do. So where does this pain that is so common come from?

The situation we've just looked at above offers one useful example. Daddy is angry—too angry. If this child is a Unicorn, he finds closeness to Daddy very frightening and painful. This will set up a lifetime of wariness around the experience of being close. If the child is a Lion, he will assume that he is flawed in some personal way, otherwise Daddy would be happy and not mad.

The pain of being *threatened* or *shamed* in this way is nearly beyond measure. Children have an absolute need to have their own preciousness reflected back to them by their parents. This mirroring must be unconditional. The more conditions attached to the process, the more conditioned the mind of the child becomes. Conditional love leaves in its wake conditioning in the form of (1) pain and (2) layers of defenses that offer protection from that pain.

The first outcome of such conditioning is that our powers of perception and feeling collaborate to form one "part," the part that carries the pain of having certain needs unmet in our first childhood relationship. For many Lions, the perception is "nobody cares." The feeling that goes along with the "perception" that nobody cares is a form of shame—usually rejection. So the painful feeling of rejection goes through life hand-in-hand with a perception that nobody cares. Other words that Lions use to describe their pain are unloved, unacceptable, uncared for, unappreciated, and disregarded. This is simply because they personalize any breakdown in the First Relationship—that is, they attribute the breakdown(s) in that relationship to faults in themselves rather than in the other person, albeit they may have no idea what those faults in themselves may be.

Unicorns, in contrast, often color their world with the perception that there is a "threat of conflict," or a "threat of rejection" or "potential for failure to make the other person happy." The feeling that goes along with this "perception" is anxiety or fear. Other perceptions that many Unicorns report are "Here we go again," or "walking on eggshells" or "Nothing I do will work." Unicorns describe the painful feeling as pressure, discomfort, emptiness, hollowness, fear, nervousness, a sense of dread, and anxiety.

This part that carries the pain of our first childhood relationship is the black sheep of our internal system. We don't want to feel this pain. We don't want to acknowledge it. We don't want to see it. Yet if we do, we will find a small child sitting alone waiting for us, for *someone*, to come.

It is difficult to look at our angry wife or our burly husband and see the little girl or boy that lives inside of them. Why is this so difficult? It's because we have never met the little boy or girl that lives inside of ourselves, so naturally we can't imagine such a child inside anyone else. It's hard to remember that the man who is big and strong was once a tiny little guy who just wanted his father's love or the safety of closeness with his mother. Imagine that attractive, articulate mother of two as a child desperate for approval from an absent father or thrust between fighting alcoholic parents.

I remember one client who was trying to imagine meeting this part of himself. As he conjured up the image of his pain, a little boy stepped forward who looked exactly like him. My client's eyes got big and he looked at me, proclaiming that inside he had discovered "mini me!"

A question arises: Is this part—or any part, for that matter—just a metaphor for an aspect of our personality or is it a fully developed person, a singularity? I believe that parts are intact and complete in and of themselves. They live inside, stuck in the world they knew when they were first born, during that first relationship. That is the world they perceive. As long as we sleep the deep sleep of being on automatic pilot and letting our Limbic System run our lives, our pain colors every moment of our perception.

The Protector

We've seen how the first two steps of the cognitive process: perception and feeling produce a part whose function is to carry a certain kind of pain throughout our life. What about defensive behavior? Do we also form a part whose function is to defend against feeling that pain? Yes, we do. I call that part the "Protector."

The part that defends is another singularity or full personality. Its job is to protect the little boy or little girl who is in pain. This is usually an angry or resentful part. But it can as well be a part that uses drugs or alcohol to douse the pain. This part will even resort to suicide to protect from too much pain.

This is the angry teenager of the internal system. I say this because often a client will visualize this part as a teenaged version of him- or herself. Why a teenager? Because, as almost anyone who has raised one will quickly support, anger truly emerges during those years.

Sometimes the angry defensive part is described as a warrior or fighter. Many times it wears a suit of armor. No matter the description, the job of this part is clear: Immediately and energetically protect the part that carries the pain.

What is interesting about this is that the little child in pain part is deathly afraid of the anger. It knows that the cost of protection is likely destruction. Protectors don't care, however. They will do whatever it takes

75

to shield the person from feeling their pain, including blow up their life if necessary.

Just as people do not want to feel their pain, they do not want to acknowledge their anger. They just want to get rid of it. When I tell them they must love it, they look at me as if I'm crazy. But until we embrace the part or parts of us that mean to protect us, we will never gain control of our internal milieu. When I take a client to meet that part of themselves, the first question I ask is: "What is the positive intention this part has for your life?"

Many times, they question me. "Positive? Are you sure?" When they learn that the angry part is merely trying to protect them, they are surprised. This, of course, is especially true for Lions. Since their anger tends to be so much in their face they view it as the single most negavtive part of their personality.

In the case of Unicorns, the tactic used by the part that defends is not anger but avoidance. This part that avoids conflict has similar goals to its angry counterpart in Lions. The goal is protection from feeling emotional pain. Running is effective protection. That's why the urge to run can be so strong.

Parts that are singularities residing in the Limbic System sound fantastic, doesn't it? Well, I actually see them every day. And so will you if you get this idea. It's really not esoteric at all. Let me give you a glimpse of how easy these parts are to spot in therapy.

It/s not unusual for someone in their first session to cry as they talk about the parent at the center of their first "relationship." They gladly accept my offer of a tissue to dab their eyes as they soothe their own pain. Then they turn to me angrily and say, "Oh, my God, I'm crying. I told myself I wouldn't cry when I came to see you. I hate crying. I *never* cry!"

What I have before me is someone who does not want to see their pain. As the wounded part emerges with its strong emotions, the Protector part is supremely threatened and immediately steps in to stop and condemn the behavior. When things calm down, the Protector, along with its anger, recedes and a new persona steps forward to continue the conversation as if nothing happened. During the course of such a session, I watch the person shift from one part to another, often in mid-sentence as the they struggle to make sense of their situation from these multiple points of view.

Strivers, the Defensive Theme

It is logical to ask if there is another part that controls the Limbic System when the person is not either feeling their pain or actively defending. The answer is yes. I call this part the "Striver." The Striver's job is the third of the basic functions: to strive to solve the problem of the pain. It also tries to prevent the person from actually feeling the pain that is being carried.

Sometimes we have more than one Striver. Strivers are a form of protection but differ in the way they emerge in a person's life. While Protector parts come out to get rid of the pain by avoiding or displaying anger in response to a particular incident, Strivers like to pretend that they are the actual person most of the time. In other words, they tend to masquerade as us, the real person. Protection is a reaction, striving is a life theme or lifestyle. Oftentimes, people are so attached to their Striver role that they have no real identity outside of it. Let's look at the cognitive model again with this new information.

Figure 8-2 Our lifestyle is an outgrowth of our internal process.

Here's how the process might work in a typical Lion:

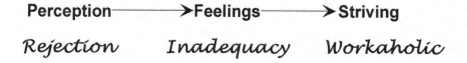

Figure 8-3 A possible lifestyle

Remember, Lions take things personally and need lots of approval. So they live in a world that finds them unacceptable, "less than." A world where no one cares. In short, they feel inferior, inadequate, and carry a sense of shame. What are they going to do about it? In this case: work, achieve, accomplish, accumulate, and strive. Workaholism becomes they lifestyle choice they use as a defensive behavior. They don't know it, but underneath it all they are trying to prove to their "relationship" that they are good enough. We'll look into this "relationship"—what and who it is and where it comes from—in chapter ten.

You might say, "Hey, I know Unicorns who are workaholics, too. What about them?" Good point. Remember, though, that Unicorns are driven by fear. In that case, *fear* of being inadequate replaces *feelings* of inadequacy. Either fear or shame can drive workaholism.

Let's think for a moment about the purpose of the striving behavior. It's really twofold. First, if we're busy working, we never have to feel the pain, do we? Staying busy, working, keeping ourselves distracted from what's really inside of us—this kind of behavior works really well for that. Second, if we achieve enough we won't be seen as inadequate, thereby extinguishing the pain or at least compensating for it. We have enough achievement notched on our career belt that the world *has* to respect us. Or, in the case of a Unicorn, the insulation that success brings is a barrier of protection from an unpredictable and chaotic world.

How about another example of a defensive theme?

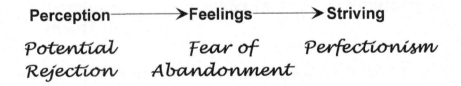

Perception ──────➤ Feelings ────────➤ Striving

Potential   Fear of   Perfectionism
Rejection   Abandonment

Figure 8-4 Another defensive lifestyle

This is a typical Unicorn pattern. In this case, life is about the constant threat of "the relationship" not being there. The conclusion: Be perfect. Striving to be perfect means if I pull it off, I won't be rejected. This can manifest itself in several forms of striving: the perfect hostess, the perfect Mom, the perfect worker, the good one, the one who follows all the rules, the one who never does anything bad. (Try to make hot monkey love to the "good" one. There's a prickly proposition).

The most common defensive themes or lifestyles I see are The Achiever, The Perfectionist, The Workaholic, The Know-It-All, The Self-Reliant One, and The Caretaker. Others include: The Worrier, The Denier, The Entitled One, The Pseudo-Intellectual, The Critic, The "I'm Right" One, The Victim, The Vigilant One, The Passive Pessimist, The Complainer, and The Defeated One.

Don't Think of Purple Cows

Suppose I told you, "Don't think of purple cows." Now that's pretty ridiculous, isn't it? But I'll wager that not one person who looked at those words did not immediately think of a purple cow. Oh, except "the know-it-all" in Riverside, California, who just said to himself, "Well, I didn't think of it."

The simple fact is that in order to not think of purple cows, you must first think of one. As long as you're struggling not to think of it, you must of necessity develop a purple cow consciousness. In other words, a purple cow must be lurking in the back of your mind in order *not* to think of it. It's a paradox. In order not to think of it, you must think of it. The same is true of our parts that give us our defensive themes. Striving is the result of trying and trying is the result of the paradox.

Consider the example of the workaholic who is striving to prove that he or she is not inadequate. In order to prove they are not inadequate, their mind has to constantly work against a backdrop of inadequacy. In essence, they must continue to recreate the experience of what they are working to get rid of. This becomes like a background feeling tone. It's always there. It is so pervasive in a person's life that their thoughts literally stink of it. Yet they are so used to having this thing in the background of their every thought that they no longer notice it.

When you learn to listen carefully to everything a person says, as a therapist is supposed to do, you literally hear the person screaming their pain in every breath. It is the backdrop for much of what they express, even about the weather.

What this sets up is thematic striving to overcome something continually recreated in the very act of trying to overcome it. This ongoing dynamism is the paradox of the human condition.

That Which We Disown

The parts of us we don't want to see or acknowledge I call "disowned" parts. They go by other names, too, like "the shadow." Poet and bestselling author, Robert Bly, calls the shadow "the long bag we drag behind us." In *A Little Book on the Human Shadow*, he describes the process like this:

> . . . one day we notice that our parents didn't like certain
> parts of that ball (us). They say things like: "Can't you be still?"
> Or "It isn't nice to try and kill your brother." Behind us we
> have an invisible bag, and the part of us our parents don't like,

79

we, to keep our parents' love, put in the bag. By the time we go to school our bag is quite large. Then our teachers have their say: "Good children don't get angry over such little things." So we take our anger and put it in the bag. By the time my brother and I were twelve in Madison, Minnesota, we were known as "the nice Bly boys." Our bags were already a mile long.

No one has more eloquently described the formation of disowned parts. What is a disowned part? Before, we were talking about the part of us that carries pain and the part that protects us. The disowned part is a little more amorphous than they are. This notion is a metaphor for the aspect of ourselves that we don't want to see. So what we do is project it on our partner and then object like hell that they have it.

In the case of Lions and Unicorns, this dynamic falls into a predictable pattern. Since Lions present themselves as pillars of strength, what they don't want to see about themselves isn't much of a mystery: the opposite of strength. Weakness? Right!

Lions hate their own sense of weakness and vulnerability. We all have an objection to seeing our pained part. Since that part of us is a small, helpless, little child, Lions don't like seeing that in themselves at all. There's nothing small and helpless about a Lion. Projecting that helpless smallness onto their Unicorn partner is a cinch: The Unicorn defense is a passive defense. They are often on the run. To a Lion, this behavior looks like the ultimate in weakness and cowardice. What the Lion will do, then, is to project their own weakness and vulnerability onto their Unicorn partner, then hate and attack what they "see" in the other person.

Unicorns, on the other hand, are the peaceniks of the relationship. Since they crave safety, comfort, and harmony, the last thing they ever want to acknowledge is their own anger, violence, and hostility. It turns out (another news flash, for some?) that the human race, and each individual in it, has a mind filled with violence and hostility. The other day, for example, I had a female Unicorn in my office. At one point she retorted, "Bullshit." I turned to her and said, "Imagine the amount of hostility that fills a mind prompting a comment like that." She looked at me as if I had lost my mind, so adamant are Unicorns not to see their own lack of peace.

Well, this is a perfect setup. Since Lions roar, they get to be the angry ones in the relationship. Pretty soon they're not only acting out their own anger but all of the anger being projected onto them by their Unicorn partner. By the time they get to therapy, the Lion is the crazy, angry, bad one in the relationship and the Unicorn is cleverly playing the role of sane, reasonable, and calm.

To sum up, then: Lions disown their weakness and vulnerability and Unicorns disown their anger and hostility. Each in their own way projects that which they disown onto their partner. In turn they use the presence of those qualities in the partner as justification for attack after attack, and an endless cycle of blaming and recriminations.

While I see this pattern repeatedly, occasionally there is a divergence— as with Lisa in the previous chapter. If a Unicorn is pushed severely enough during their developmental years, they can be taught to disown their weakness and vulnerability. What is interesting about this is that, in those cases, they will go out and find a Lion who has a habit of playing the role of the victim in some way. In other words, if a Lion is acting out their woundedness in some new or novel fashion, a Unicorn who objects to it will find them and marry them.

Parenthetically I see these aberrations in other areas. For instance, a Unicorn who is an extravert will find a Lion who is an introvert. And the beat goes on. It seems that whenever there is a reversal of an expected relational pattern, the partner has the opposite reversal. It's eerie to watch, sometimes. The mystery is how we manage to find one another. We are only beginning to understand the depth of human perception and communication. Frankly, I think our communication, body language, facial expressions, and a host of other personal details, loudly broadcast who we are and what we are seeking. We hone in on one another like magnets that soon get close enough that they slam together, in an emotional force field that compels us to stick to one another.

Evidence of this is now coming from science. For the first year or more of life, a child learns to activate and regulate levels of arousal by gazing at the mother. This is done through the orbital frontal cortex of the nonverbal right hemisphere. The child literally learns to decode the mother's Central Nervous System which is visible through her gaze and facial expression. This nonverbal communication is so highly evolved that the right orbital frontal cortex is larger than the left. This ability is developed extensively, long before we utter our first words.

This ability to decode gaze patterns which in turn arouse our own Central Nervous System stays with us through a life time. The reason we aren't more consciously aware of it is that it all is processed in the nonverbal right hemisphere of the brain.

So it is entirely plausible that without knowing it our faces become billboards for our emotional pain and defense that attracts someone with complimentary issues.

Chapter 9

Through a Glass Darkly

Angie Observes Her Anger

"I've tried to study my anger," Angie says, "I'm angry all the time!"

"So, Pat, what have you noticed about yourself?" I ask him. "Angie seems to have tuned into her anger. What's going on with you?" We have devoted several sessions to working through each person's "process," and they're beginning to understand.

At first, laid out neatly on the whiteboard, these principles look so simple. Taking them into everyday awareness training is hard, though. To borrow from an old song: "Waking up is hard to do." It really boils down to figuring out how to cut through the mist that has accumulated during some thirty years, in this case, of unconscious, automatic living.

An extreme example of what's involved in this waking up is very much like what we might see in one of those trashy talk shows on TV. We in the audience can see the people on the stage clearly. They're throwing folding chairs. They're sleeping with each other's mother, or dog, or family priest. One has a crush on the other's trailer. We in the audience can see clearly that all the people on stage have mental and emotional problems.

My goal in therapy is to get my clients off their stage and into the audience, so they can see what they're doing and how they do it. We might call it "being outside of yourself." I call it shifting into the prefrontal lobes, because from that part of the brain we can actually "see" the Limbic System and all of the drama it has going on. In psychology, the term for this "seeing" is *self-referencing*. In eastern thought, we hear the term *self-observation*. Whatever we call it, we're talking about the ability of the greater self to see the little selves. We have in the prefrontal lobes a meta-self, or a self above the other selves, that can watch the parts of the Limbic System running around and doing their automatic self-preserving behaviors that they learned in childhood.

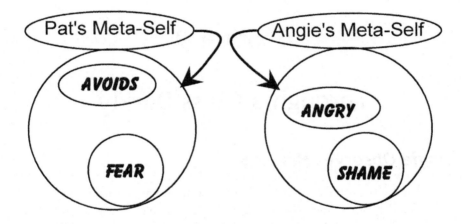

Figure 9-1 The Frontal Lobes (meta-self) can observe the Limbic System

I turn to Angie and say, "Give me an example of your anger. But pick a relatively small incident so we can work through it."

"Okay." She thinks for a minute and then says, "Friday night." Pat sighs and rolls his eyes.

"Tell me about Friday night," I urge.

"Well, in the morning we talked about getting together for a special date night. Pat said he would be home at about 6:00. He didn't show up, and at about 6:30 I started to call his cell phone. I couldn't get an answer. I must have called about ten times. He never returned my call or answered his phone. I didn't think he got any of my messages." She reaches for a tissue and dabs the corners of her eyes.

"When did he get home?" I ask.

"I got home at around 7:00. It was no big deal. God, Angie, everything is such a big deal."

"Wait a minute, Pat. Don't defend just yet. Let's see what really happened here. Shall we?"

Pat shrugs and Angie nods.

"Oh, I know what happened. I got angry. I could see myself getting angry, but I just couldn't seem to control it. I knew I felt that he just didn't care about me. In between calls to his cell phone, I would sit like you told me to do and see myself getting angry. I could! But I couldn't control it." She begins to sob, turns to Pat, and says, "I'm sorry. I'm so sorry."

Pat looks a little stricken. He hands Angie another tissue.

"Pat, what's it like being with her when she's like this."

"It's hard. I don't want to see her in so much pain. I didn't think being a little late was that big of a deal."

"I know, Pat. But what's the feeling that you are having right now? What do you want to do?"

"I guess I want to comfort her. I never realized how much her feelings get hurt."

Compassion is the fuel of intimacy and I want them to have an intimate moment so I get out of my chair. "Go ahead and comfort her right now. I've got to visit the rest room for a moment." As I leave the room, I wonder if this is the first time Pat has truly seen Angie's pain.

I return to the counseling room a few minutes later. Angie has composed herself and Pat has a satisfied look that indicates he has achieved his ongoing goal—peace at last.

"Now, Angie, with your permission I would like to process through Pat's side of all this. Would that be okay?"

She indicates that she's okay with that, so I proceed. "Pat, what's your story about Friday night?"

"Well, we had a visit from our VP on Friday and he wanted to take the crew out for a beer after work. I knew it wouldn't take too long. I didn't think it would be a big deal. I know I should have called. I guess I thought I could get home in time so it wouldn't be a big deal."

"You know, Pat, I think it's time you faced what really goes on inside of you. I think you didn't call because you knew it would be a 'big deal.' Isn't that true? Let's put up our little process diagram again and go through it."

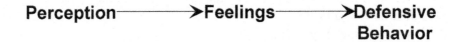

Figure 9-2 The Internal Process

"Now, Pat, when you realized you were going to be late, what was the first thing that went through your mind?"

"I thought, 'Oh shit, how do I get out of this one?'" Pat put his hand over his eyes as if he didn't want to see what was coming next.

"Did it occur to you to call Angie and let her know what was happening?"

"Oh, yeah, but I knew she would just lose it."

"Pat, did it seem to you that, no matter what you did, Angie would be unhappy and you would be in the dog house?"

Pat smiled a grim smile of resignation. "Oh, yeah."

"So here's Pat thinking 'Here we go again, I can't win, I'm in the dog house?'"

"That's pretty much it. There's a storm a'comin' and there's nowhere to run!"

"Well, I think that pretty much sums up your perception. No matter what you did there was going to be conflict, right?"

"Right. Oh, and I know the next question you're going to ask: How did that make me feel? Well, check it out, I felt awful, sick to my stomach. God, if I knew that was what therapy was going to do I would never have come. I was damn near sick to my stomach with anxiety for two hours."

I smile. It's always my fault. Now he's in touch with how he really feels and he's really feeling it, and it's my fault. "So, Pat, that's great. I see you have tuned in to the feeling. That's very important. So what was your defensive behavior?"

"I didn't have any. I had a couple of beers, and when the coast was clear, I headed home."

"Pat, listen to yourself. 'When the coast was clear?' You have to be kidding. Can you hear the fear in that expression? Your defensive behavior is obvious. You assumed that no matter what you did, it wouldn't work. All paths lead to conflict. Am I right?" Pat nods. "So you did nothing. That's called avoiding. You figured that if you did nothing you might get lucky and avoid a fight. Avoiding is your defensive behavior."

Pat looks at me with resignation. "Yeah, I guess you're right. I do it all the time, don't I?"

"Yes, you do. The moment you thought about calling Angie, that anxiety about possible conflict came up, and you defended immediately by not calling. It's so automatic that you do it without thinking. That has to change. You have to allow yourself to notice what you're doing. Let's go back to the process diagram now. I'm going to put down 'threat of conflict,' but notice that it's the same perception that gave us 'out of control' when we drew this up here before. When there is conflict, things are out of control. Right?"

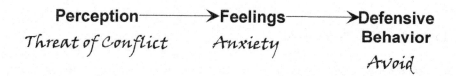

Figure 9-3 Pat's Process

"Now I'm going to change the drawing a little so we can look at the perception a little differently. I'm not much of an artist, so here goes."

I work away at drawing a little stick figure and then label it "Angie." "Sorry, Angie, that's the best I can do."

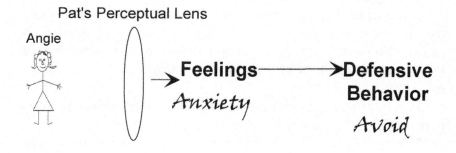

Figure 9-4 Pat's Perception

Now, what happens to light when it goes through a lens?"

Angie pipes up, "It splits into the colors of the rainbow."

Pat laughs a little and says, "No, Hon, that would be a prism, not a lens. For a lens the light rays are bent."

"Right, Pat. And they may actually turn the image upside down." I add a little more to my drawing.

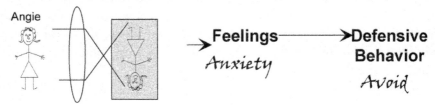

Figure 9-5 What Pat's lens does

"All right! I shouldn't quit my day job. What we see here is that when Pat 'perceives' Angie, his distorted perceptual lens turns Angie into something or someone else. Maybe a better term would be the word "morphed" —in Pat's mind under this circumstance, Angie morphs into someone or something else. Remember that the Limbic System causes this distortion—specifically, the emotional reactivity of the Amygdala and the memory function of the Hippocampus. They team up to give a perception based on some association from the past that has a similar emotional content. Possibly this is what the apostle Paul meant when he said. 'We see through a glass darkly.'"

I turn to Pat and say, "Think for a minute, Pat. There's going to be conflict. You're in a no-win situation. You can't run. You can't hide. No matter what you do, there will be an explosion of emotion—probably rage. Who comes to mind? What face do you immediately see in your mind's eye?"

Pat's face suddenly flushes and he looks me in the eye with an expression of horror. "Dad," he says, in almost a whisper.

"Right, Dad." I draw a dotted line on the board and now the picture is complete.

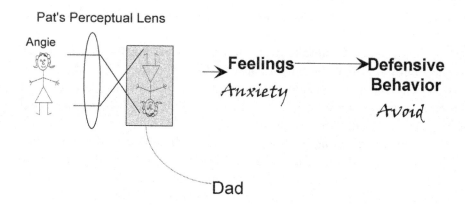

Figure 9-6 What Pat really sees

"Oh, my God!" cries Angie.

"What Pat's Limbic System has done is to turn Angie into Dad, which triggers massive amounts of anxiety, leading him to avoid the situation at all costs."

Pat looks at the board, then at me. "Do I really do that?"

"Yes, you do. You do it so quickly and so often—and you're so used to doing it—that you don't even notice it. Yet it happens repeatedly. You live in a world where you're constantly protecting yourself from Dad. Dad isn't even here any more, but your primitive brain doesn't know that. It thinks that anyone who is intimate with you must be Dad, so it helps you with a strategy designed just for that."

Angie points a crooked finger at the board. "I'm doing it too, aren't I? I morph him into my father."

"Yes, you do, Angie. We all do it. The key to freedom is to *notice* yourself doing it. Each of us picks the 'relationship' with either our father or mother. Then we organize our strivings and defenses around the pain that emerges in that relationship. Those strategies become the organizing principles we use to run relationships."

Ghosts of Those I Couldn't Help

Robert and Lindiqua have come to see me for the first time. Over the phone, it seemed that the issue was her spending habits and the fact that he was ready for a divorce. Just based on that small amount of information,

I already had a good idea of who was who and what was what in the relationship.

Analyzing it is simple. If my spouse is spending too much money, she might appear to be out of control. "Out of control" is a phrase that describes a Unicorn's perception that in its turn would spark a lot of fear in them. So in my mind I have a picture of this man who is being terrorized by his wife's being "out of control."

Excessive spending or shopping, on the other hand, is also a behavior driven by emotions. Most spender/shopper types, whether they are women in the mall or men in the electronics store, are attempting to make themselves feel better. So in my mind's eye, before Robert and Lindiqua arrive in my office, I see a woman trying to feel better (shame) and a man experiencing large doses of fear. In other words, I have guessed that he is the Unicorn and she is the Lion.

As they enter my office, Robert immediately slumps into one of the chairs and looks at me with a dull glare. He's a Unicorn, all right. He has retreated so far back into his defenses that I'm not sure I can ever draw him out. Lindiqua has a downcast look and avoids eye contact.

"So, what can I do for the two of you?"

Lindiqua lifts her head. "He says I spend too much so he wants a divorce."

I turn to him and ask, "Is that true?"

"She just won't take responsibility. I really don't care anymore."

What comes out in our discussion is that they've been married for ten years. For ten years she has been "irresponsible" and he has stuffed his feelings about it. Recently, however, his feeling won't stay stuffed any more. It's clear from looking at Robert that he has given up, shut down completely, and is extremely resentful. He's done. This man is what I call a visitor, not a candidate for becoming a client.

I ask Lindiqua, "So what's your complaint about Robert?"

"He's never there."

"How does that make you feel?"

"Alone, unwanted."

"Kind of rejected?"

She nods as if I've just hit the nail on the head.

I have before me a classic case of the Lion/Unicorn scenario just as I had anticipated. The real question is Can I help them. Robert acts very disconnected. Lindiqua is disconsolate. This is not a good situation.

After we discuss their relationship for a while, I say, "Let me ask you a little about your backgrounds. Would that be okay?"

They nod and I plunge ahead. "Robert, tell me a little about your family history?"

What comes out is not pretty. At four years old, he witnessed his drug-addicted father shoot and kill his mother's brother. His father ended up in prison, and Robert spent much of the rest of his young life with his uncle on his father's side. His uncle was an alcoholic whose parties with other relatives and members of the extended family ended in brawls, with the occasional stabbing or shooting. His mother was an angry, volatile woman whose idea of a conversation easily escalated into screaming or shouting.

In short, Robert had an early life filled with violence and chaos. When I ask how he feels about that and how it might have affected him, he says, "I don't think all the fighting was necessary."

That is the kind of Unicorn answer I expected. The man is totally shut down, hiding deep within himself. Five times during his report of his childhood he recounted horrible events, and when I asked how they made him feel, he never once responded with a feeling; every answer was an evasion.

Lindiqua's story is no less tragic. She was raised in a violent, alcoholic family. Mom and Dad fought and damaged furniture and property much of her young life. She says her role in the family was to protect her Mother when Dad would attack. There she was, as early as the age of four, in the middle of two violent parents. This would have been bad enough. But when things calmed down, neither parent took the time to tell her she was wanted, needed, acceptable, or special in any way. When I ask her about the feeling that went along with that, she is able to access a lot of rejection, identified with her father.

At this point, near the end of the session, I draw a ragged breath and look at them. The amount of damage done to them during childhood is significant. Because of the large amount of violence they have seen, the Limbic System of each of them has adapted to massive amounts of stress. Of course, since she is a Lion and he is a Unicorn, their reaction to their stress was entirely different.

My problem here is simple and nearly unsolvable. I have to get them to continue coming. But he seems completely checked out. There's almost no way he'll come back. During the session I have drawn circles, I have explained what's happening in their relationship. I hope something I've said or done shows them what's really at work.

The chances are that what I've offered is too little and too late. Helping them reverse the damage done to them would require inspired participation by both of them over a long period. That appears to be unlikely.

I walk them to the door of my office and encourage them to call me, as Robert has refused to make another appointment until he thinks more about it. He knows my goal will be to save the marriage. I can feel his resistance to that goal. He's done. Mentally he has left already. In a cruel way, their defenses have escorted them back to the predicament of childhood. Robert retreats in terror from the constant disappointment of the person he loves, while Lindiqua suffers the ultimate abandonment she has struggled so hard to avoid.

I leave the office and drive home to my private life. Their ghosts are in the back seat of my car.

Chapter 10

Projection and the Shadow from the Past

We saw in chapter nine one way that distortion drives emotional reactivity in a relationship: We "see" something that isn't there. We're so used to "seeing" it that operating with this distorted perception has become second nature.

Think about it for a moment. If we all see something that isn't there, that means we must be projecting that thing from inside our heads. Projection, then, is the function of making something up and beaming it out of our heads onto an otherwise unsullied reality.

Projection is more than just misunderstanding what someone else is saying. That would be too easy. If that were the case, I could just teach "communication skills" and everything would be all better. When a wife says, "Good morning" to her husband and he growls back, "What's good about it?" we might assume that he heard something in her voice that carried more meaning for him. Maybe he thought he heard sarcasm or a put-down; maybe he mentally tacked "asshole" onto the end of the greeting.

If this were the case, we could straighten that problem out right away. It is easy to understand how anger and resentment might color our perceptions over a long period of time. But there is more to this process of projection, much more.

When a child becomes a person with "I am" awareness and identifies that as "this person in this body," they attempt to participate in a relationship.

What happens in that relational space imprints the child brain with the "principles" of an intimate relationship. And it does far more than that. Yes, we learn a series of steps, principles, and concepts. However, we also learn to whom we are relating.

This "whom" is a specific person at that point in the child's development. It is the person chosen by the child and onto whom they focus relational energy. This is nearly always Mom or Dad (although, it could be an older sibling if there is a significant age difference, and if one or the other of the parents is not present). This chosen person will become "the relationship" that the Limbic System will always see, no matter how old we are or how far we travel from home. The child's primitive brain learns one, and only one, relationship.

You grow up and get married, but it makes no difference. After the honeymoon, the relationship gradually goes on autopilot and, since the Limbic System is our autopilot, we act as if we're still in that early relationship. The Limbic System has learned just that one relationship, and it is determined that that is the only relationship you will ever have. As soon as anyone crosses the boundary into that intimate space, the Limbic System reacts accordingly by casting the shadow of Mom or Dad (or your substitute for them) across the current person.

As spooky as it sounds, relationships become nothing more than a stage on which you and your shadow figure continue the painful struggle that was set up in the distant past. The focus of the child's brain becomes attempting to satisfy the needs that were not met in that original relationship. Your current partner is a shill in a sick game to attempt to heal your own heart.

The Result of THE Relationship

Let's go back to that original relationship from the perspective of the Lion and the Unicorn, to see which kinds of parents produce which kinds of pain. As I write this, I realize that I am blaming parents for causing their children's emotional pain. And to a large extent, this is true. We hear the term "the abuse excuse" in the media as if abusing children is not a determinant in future behavior. I would invite the experts, talking heads, and commentators to go into any prison and listen to the personal history of the inmates. Or to talk to some mental health professionals who listen to people's histories all day long. The simple fact is that the way we raise children is fraught with physical, sexual, and emotional abuse and neglect.

What do children need? They need limits and boundaries consistently enforced with reasonable consequences that relate to the desired behavior. They need validation, not value judgments. Corporal punishment is okay as long as it is mild and never done as acting out anger. Yelling, blaming, name calling, threats, and the like damage the parent-child relationship and teach the child that the route to fulfillment is through dealing with insanity.

The Unicorn

Unicorns need safety. They need their own space, and they need their own natural reticence honored. They hate chaotic environments. That is excessively threatening. The Unicorn child will nearly always pick the parent who is in their face as "the relationship." From the raging father to the emotionally needy mother, the one thing the Unicorn learns is that nothing they will do will ever make the other person happy. If they try and fail they will be rejected which is extremely frightening for a four- or five-year-old Unicorn. If they aren't rejected they will be yelled at, which is extremely uncomfortable to the Unicorn.

Therefore, their life comes down to "handling" this volatile person. The first stage of defense is to make themselves unavailable physically and emotionally. This is avoidance. It is typical for a Unicorn to shut down when you ask any question of consequence. They are inside wondering, what if I get the answer wrong? They will literally disappear emotionally right before your eyes.

After a period in the family, they will stay shut down. Their theory is if they stay invisible and unavailable, there will be less of them showing to provoke an attack.

The second line of defense is to promise and placate or even take care of the other person's feelings. Most male Unicorns know a lot about the fine art of making promises designed solely to get the other person off their backs. They will even lie. This lying and promising, since it is insincere, leaves the other person the impression that the Unicorn can't be trusted. This is not true. They are trustworthy. They just don't feel safe and they don't want to be smothered by the emotional demands of the other person. Psychologists call this fear of engulfment.

Female Unicorns learn the fine art of caretaking. They will do anything to make you happy; rub your back, quit their job, whatever it takes to have peace and safety. They become good little housekeepers, codependent, seemingly caring. That's not to say that these roles are always gender specific.

If they can't avoid or placate, they feel cornered. You do not want a Unicorn near you when they feel cornered, because they will come out swinging. At this point, they can be more dangerous than any Lion.

The bottom line is a relationship image built into the Limbic System that is about dealing with someone who is patriarchal, emotionally demanding, threatening, an in-your-face kind of parent. This sets up a scenario that tells the Unicorn that relationships are about the constant struggle for freedom, space, and air with someone who cannot be made happy, who is intrusive, prying, and demanding. The very thought of this relationship injects large quantities of adrenaline into the flight or fight system.

This is a shame since Unicorns, underneath it all, like Lions, have a desperate primal need for closeness and intimacy. Throughout their lives, they will continue to seek closeness only to push it away as the emotional toll of trying to do mounts inside.

The Lion

The Lion child needs approval, not shame. They typically pick the parent whom they see as withholding approval. Oftentimes this comes in the form of a parent who is physically and/or emotionally unavailable. Or it comes in the form of a parent who is shaming and critical, who sends the message that "nothing you do is ever good enough." This sets up a lifelong struggle to try to get the approval, recognition, acceptance, and love that the Lion never got in this first relationship.

How does the Lion deal with the critical or uncaring parent? Defiance. The Unicorn's reaction to unmet safety needs is despair. The Lion's reaction to unmet needs for acceptance and encouragement is defiance. A power struggle will be the result between the young Lion and the parent.

The damage to the Lion child from having a disapproving or uninvolved parent is immense. Everything becomes personal. This kind of experience can lead to a perception of not belonging, not being included. Everything becomes a slight of some kind or another.

A Look at Twins

All researchers do twin studies. Identical twins are thought to have identical natures, so that what happens in the family leads to developmental differences, which in turn account for the differences between twins.

Let's do a little hypothetical twin study of our own. In our study, we'll assume that Mutt and Jeff, our mythical twins, are fraternal rather than identical. Not only are they non-identical, but Mutt is a Unicorn and Jeff is a Lion. Other than that, their lives are identical in every respect.

Like many of us, they were born into a dysfunctional family system. In this case, their father is a traveling salesman who is almost never home and their mother is an alcoholic who is erratic, unpredictable, and emotionally unreliable.

Life is not good for Mutt and Jeff. By the time they're in kindergarten, they're latchkey kids. Mom, who is dealing with a daily hangover, forces them out of the house in the morning. When they come home from school at around noon, no one is there until late in the evening.

The conversation between Mutt and Jeff upon arriving home from school goes something like this:

"Jeff, there's no one home again. What'll we do?"

"Do? Do what ever we want. They don't care," Jeff says defiantly.

"Yeah, but there's no food in the refrigerator. What are we supposed to eat?" Mutt whines.

"They want us to eat cereal or junk food. Do you think either of them actually thinks about what we might *want* for lunch when we get home?"

"They might not even come home!" cries Mutt. "Suppose they forget we're even here? We might starve!"

"Look, Mutt. If they thought we were important, they'd show up. They don't show up because we're *rejects*. As long as we watch TV and stay out of the way, they're cool."

While I admit I'm not sure what a conversation between two kindergarteners would really sound like, you can tell that Mutt and Jeff have two radically different interpretations of the events in the household.

Mutt is concerned with getting the basic needs met. He is fearful they will starve; he is concerned with ultimate abandonment. He is going to grow up with a fundamental issue that will feel something like *fear of rejection*.

Jeff has a very different view on the situation. He clearly believes that if the parents cared more they would be available to meet basic needs. His interpretation of the circumstance is that parental neglect is a personal attack on them. He is feeling *rejected*.

Notice that fear of rejection and feeling rejectable are two dramatically different feelings. One is rooted in fear or lack of safety, the other in shame or lack of approval. Given an identical circumstance, the Unicorn looks at the world through the lens of fear while the Lion looks through a lens of shame. This difference is not subtle. It is a large, glaring world shaping difference.

Identifying the Shadow Figure

How do we identify which parent is in later life the shadow figure, that parent we piced as our first relationship? This at first would seem to be a somewhat mystical process of revealing the subconscious—one that takes perhaps years of therapy. But let me show you how easily this can be accomplished by relating a session I had just last night. A young woman came to me for her first session.

I sat there for some time trying to determine whether she was a Lion or Unicorn. (I would much rather see a couple: You can tell who is who much easier.) As we talked, I noticed her references to her ex-husband's "not caring" about her and being "disrespectful." It seemed that he often would not come home at the appropriate time, a definite Unicorn characteristic of avoidance. When he did come home, they might have words and, after the argument, she would blame herself and wonder how she might strive to be better. Throughout our discussion, this "I'm not good enough" feeling kept coming up in her communication.

How did I determine that her pain was the Lion's pain of being "not good enough"? How did she embed the message in her dialogue with me? Simple. She kept saying the words "not good enough." I've learned to listen. Clients will tell you the problem explicitly without knowing they're doing it. If you listen to the words and phrases, you can see exactly what's what.

When it finally became clear that she is a Lion and her pain feels like she isn't good enough, I asked her a clear, straightforward question, "When you think of that 'not good enough' feeling, which parent comes to mind?"

Tears immediately formed in her eyes and she said her mother. Boom! Just like that, she nailed it. That feeling that we spend a lifetime defending ourselves from came from that original relationship. When we give ourselves permission to feel the feeling, we can instantly identify which parent connects to the feeling of fear or shame. Amazingly enough, discovering the shadow figure is simple. Just ask.

How Projection Works

Okay, we now have this shadow figure firmly programmed into our mind—specifically, into our Limbic System. So let's fast-forward twenty or thirty years, to when it's time to get into a marriage or other committed relationship.

The Setup

After the honeymoon (or whatever "committed relationships" have) comes the time to settle down and become taxpayers. The fun is over, and now it's time to set the stage for some serious abuse. The sick game has to be set up somehow.

The Lion starts sending, in a variety of ways, the subliminal message: "All right, since I take everything personally, I need you to treat me like shit, put me in a one-down position, and let me be the angry one in the relationship."

The Unicorn, in just as many ways, responds: "Okay by me. I think that all that anger is socially unacceptable, anyway. So, since I'm frightened of closeness, I'm going to make myself emotionally and sometimes physically unavailable. If I must, I will promise you anything to get you off my back. By the way, I may want to play the role of the victim here. Is that okay?"

"Sure," the Lion replies through the unconscious. "Since I'm a sack of excrement anyway, that fits. By the way, I have this overwhelming need to see myself as strong, so you'll have to appear weak."

The Unicorn chimes in: "Now as I understand it, you'll be playing the role of my intrusive mother and I'll be your shut-down father. Right?"

"Right," says the Lion, and they both cheer: "Let the dance begin!"

The Template for Relationships

Since the real people who fell in love and worshiped one another have at this point abdicated the relationship to their respective Limbic Systems, they can now go unconscious. The child brain, therefore, pulls out the template of Mom or Dad, places that pattern neatly over the partner, and begins to operate as if they are actually relating to the shadow figure. They literally *are* doing so from the point of view of the primitive brain.

Now every "perception" they have of one another and one another's intentions is flooded with meaning rooted in the shadow figure. Normal things take on ghostly qualities. Lateness looks like abandonment, inattention is rejection, a conversation is a direct threat, and an emotional reaction is an attack. Everything we see brings up that exiled old feeling of shame or fear. We run from fear and flush shame with anger. The dance of the Lion and Unicorn has begun. The struggle to get emotional satisfaction from Mom or Dad has begun. Again.

The two adults behind these masks are no longer visible. They have gone to sleep. The conditional love of childhood has conditioned their minds like a strong sedative. They don't think, they survive. Their partner is not a person. He or she has become an object. Objectification is perfect since we need something inanimate onto which we can project the shadow figure.

Eventually they show up in my office. I tell them their perceptions are incorrect. I tell them that what they "see" isn't really there. They can't believe me. After all, the pictures are so big and bright. They must be real. I say, no. You're hallucinating. You're manufacturing the feelings that go with what isn't really there. Your efforts to change your world will fail, because you're really defending *your own deep pain*.

They look at me shocked. Each looks back at their respective picture. It's so vivid that they reach for sunglasses. I reach for my appointment book and pray that I'll be making another entry in it for them.

Chapter 11

Compassion the Key to Healing

Pain—the Trigger for Compassion

Tommasio and Corrine own a restaurant in the area. He is a lanky man in his early thirties and she is a diminutive dark haired beauty. When they first came to me, they were separated. He was clearly a Unicorn on the run from her temperamental outbursts. They intuitively understood the principles underlying the dance of the Lion and Unicorn, and therapeutic progress proceeded rapidly.

When I work with a couple, I try to find some small disagreement or difficult interaction to work with. Encapsulated in the smallest interaction are all of the issues that need examination so healing can take place. In one session, Tommasio spoke for a few minutes about an interaction they had. He had noticed his uncomfortable feeling and had watched helplessly as he withdrew and emotionally shut down.

"Tom, let me ask you a question. What was going through your mind just before you started to shut down?"

"I was thinking, 'Here we go again.'"

"What does that tell you about yourself, Tom?"

"That I'm anticipating the worst from Corrine?"

"Gosh, it sounds like it." I'm beginning to ask him a series of questions designed to elicit the core of what drives his behavior. "If you're always trying to anticipate the worst, what does that mean about the kind of life you will lead in the future?"

Tom thinks for a moment and looks confused, "I guess I'll go crazy."

I ask him to elaborate. In my office "going crazy" is an easy response to give, since anyone who has to come to a therapist supposedly must be crazy, by definition.

"Well, I mean, things will always be dark or negative. Maybe watching Corrine to see if she is angry or not, all the time."

"What do you think you're afraid might happen if you don't anticipate the worst?"

"I'd be caught unprepared. Things might get out of control."

I nod my head. That response is consistent with what I know about Tom. While we're talking, Corrine is listening intently. I ask Tom my next question. "Tom, if things get out of control, what's the worst that could happen to you?"

"I guess we could have a big fight and she might walk out on me."

"And if she left you, what would be the consequences to you?"

Tom doesn't hesitate to answer. "I would be alone. I don't want to be alone."

"Yes, that's right, isn't it? Now I'm going to ask you a difficult question that will require you to read Corrine's mind. Okay?"

Tom nods, "I'll try."

"If things get out of control and if Corrine walks out and you're alone, what does that tell you about her beliefs about you?"

"She'll think I'm weak, a failure," he says with a questioning tone.

"Okay, what does that tell you about Corrine or people as a whole?

"People are unpredictable. One minute they're your friends and the next they're psychos."

"Tom, this is excellent. Your answers have been fantastic. I just have one more question. When you think of people as being unpredictable, what pictures or memories come up? If more than one comes up, pick the earliest."

I watch Tom think for a moment. Corrine has turned toward him and is studying his face. I have appreciated the fact that she has remained quiet throughout this exercise.

"I remember my Dad would come home after work and we would sit around the table. If I said anything he didn't like, he would force me to get under the laundry basket. The family would pretend that I was in a cage and they would sit at the table and throw food at me. I had to reach through the slats in the basket to reach the food."

Corrine's eyes are tearing up at this point.

"How old were you when this happened?" I ask.

"About four. If I tried to get out of the 'prison,' Dad would yell and rage at me. Sometimes he would hit me."

"What about your mother?"

"Mom was pretty passive."

I let this story settle for a minute or two. Then I speak again. "Tom, I want you to understand clearly that the sheer terror of being raised like that never leaves your mind. It is omnipresent. At some level, your interactions with your wife are being dictated by a little boy who is in fear of being rejected by the family."

I turn to Corrine. "You see, Corrine, this has never been personal. This man is terrified that if you 'get out of control,' his whole world will collapse. The terrified little boy inside of him doesn't know the difference between you and his Dad. The threat is the same and the consequences are just as dire."

She reaches out and grabs Tom's hand. "I see that. I see it clearly. Tom, I never knew."

He manages a smile. "I guess I never knew either."

The conversation drifts on to more clarification. This has been a real breakthrough for both of them. He finally understands what I've been drawing on the board all these weeks. She has finally seen the real person that she married.

He turns to me as the hour expires and says, "I feel that Corrine finally knows me. I'm learning to know myself. But I don't feel that I know her. How can I get to know the real her?"

I smile broadly. "Tom, your question is its own answer in a way. Since you have finally seen your own pain, you now want to see hers. You would never have wanted to see all the painful parts of Corrine if you hadn't been willing to go to that dark threatening place inside yourself. Congratulations. This has been a huge step for both of you."

True Pain Is Like a Magnet

I'm waiting for Pat and Angie to arrive. At this stage, therapy becomes a real pleasure. The couple finally has the vision of where I'm coming from. They have the road map with which to track their personal internal process.

They know there are forces inside of each of them that are thwarting their efforts to have a successful relationship, and they're working together to wrestle control of their marriage back from the ghosts of the past.

They arrive and sit in front of me. There seems to be some peace in the room for the first time. We exchange pleasantries and I ask how it's going.

Pat seems pleased with himself. "Can I start?" He asks Angie and me. "Please, go ahead."

"The other day we were getting on the freeway, and as soon as we started down the ramp I could see that traffic was all backed up. As I saw it, I could literally feel myself close up, kind of fade away inside."

I smile broadly. Self-observation is the first step to mastery.

"Anyway, I had the presence of mind to ask myself what I was feeling. The answer was anxiety. I could feel this really uncomfortable feeling. I knew it was anxiety the moment I looked at it. Since we were stuck in traffic, I had some time to analyze it. What was my perception? I remembered what you keep putting on the board. I had to have had a perception in order to have that uncomfortable feeling triggered."

I lean forward in my chair. "What did you notice?"

"My perception was that I was going to get yelled at for getting stuck in traffic, for making a bad choice. But what was weird was that when I checked it out inside, I could hear my Dad's voice screaming at me—real critical like."

"My, God, Pat, that's fantastic! What a huge insight."

"Since then I've noticed getting nervous all the time. And I think I can hear that angry, critical voice a lot, too."

Angie pipes up, "Pat, I thought you were mad at me. You didn't say a word all the way home." She turns to me and says, "I took it personally, didn't I?"

"You see, Angie, that was an opportunity for you to question your perception. Once you notice yourself having a reaction, it's time to feel the feeling against which the reaction is a defense. For you, you know that it's always a feeling of 'nobody cares' so you can just go inside and look for that feeling. Once you've found it, you can question your perception by asking, 'What do I think is happening?'"

"I guess that 'nobody cares' feeling is out of control, isn't it?" Angie asks with resignation in her voice.

"Why don't we try a little experiment, Angie? Do you have a good imagination, or are you a good visualizer?"

"Yeah, I think so."

"Okay, what I want you to do is to take a minute or so to relax. Pat and I will just sit here while you get quiet."

I doodle in my appointment book for a moment as the room gets quiet. "Okay, ready?"

Angie nods.

I want you to imagine a room in your mind's eye. It can be any room you want it to be. It just has to have a door so you can walk in and out of it. Also, it has to have a window so you can stand outside and look into the room. Understand?"

"I already have it; but am I supposed to go into the room?"

"No, just stand outside and look into the room through the window. Are you there?"

"Yes."

I have done this exercise many times to help people get more in touch with their pain. It comes from a colleague, Richard Schwartz, in his excellent book, *Internal Family Systems Therapy*. "Now, Angie, get a little of that 'nobody cares about me' feeling. Can you?"

She nods.

"Now inside your mind, ask that part of you that carries that 'nobody cares' feeling to go into the room. You must stay outside the room while the 'nobody cares' part goes inside the room."

"How can I do that? It's me."

"I want you to pretend that the part with that feeling is separate from you. After all, you are not your feelings. You don't feel like 'nobody cares' all the time do you? So don't analyze this. Just go with the experience. Stand outside the room and ask that part with the feeling to go into the room. Take a minute or two until you can do it."

Pat and I watch Angie carefully as she closes her eyes.

"Okay, the feeling is in the room. It's dark. I don't like it."

"Angie, this is a feeling you have spent your whole life not feeling. It won't overwhelm you. Just be patient. Now, look through the window and tell me what you see."

Angie takes a minute and then says, "I see a little girl. She's all alone. I think she's crying."

"Check inside yourself and see if it would be okay for you to go in the room with the little girl." Nearly everyone I have ever worked with identifies a child version of himself or herself when we do this exercise. Angie is true to form. I'm hopeful that we can make progress in the next few minutes.

"I'm in the room. The little girl looks like me."

"How old is the little girl?"

"She's about six. She's wearing a pink dress."

"What does she do when she sees you?"

"She's disappointed. She's crying. She says she hoped it would be Dad." A tear forms and streaks down Angie's face as she says this.

"Angie, ask her a question for me. Ask her what is it she wanted from Dad but never got?"

"She says for him to just be there. Just his presence, I guess."

"Ask her what you could give her that she never got from Dad."

"She says a hug. She wants a hug."

"Go ahead and give her a hug, then."

Angie spends some time with the little girl and finally looks at me and says, "She feels better now. I held her and reassured her."

"What else happened with you and the little girl?"

Angie begins to cry freely. She grabs for one tissue after another as she tells the story of how she used to pine for her father. She would sometimes wait at night on the front steps for him to come home. Often she had to go to bed before he arrived. If he did come home while she was up, he would ruffle her hair on his way to the sports section of the paper or his shop in the garage. He never tucked her into bed or paid much attention beyond a cursory greeting here or there. He didn't have time for her. He showed little interest. She wasn't important. Before me sat a grown woman grieving for the father who was not emotionally or often physically available to her.

Pat's face shows raw emotion as he watches Angie. He is clearly at a loss for words, but he does manage to mumble, "I didn't know. I'm sorry."

I wait until Angie has wiped away the last tear and a sense of calm settles over the three of us. "Pat, what were you feeling as Angie was experiencing all of that emotion?"

"God, I just felt bad. I never knew she hurt so much."

"Before we wrap things up today, let's talk a little about intimacy. I want to share with you something I've learned about the secret of intimacy. The reason is that Angie has encountered her pain today and, Pat, you were able to see it. And Angie, you try to remember that you watched previously when Pat had his own encounter with the pain of the past."

I go to the whiteboard and begin to draw circles. When I'm done, it looks like this:

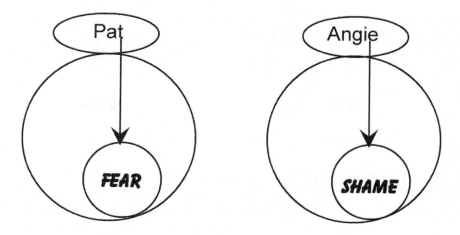

Figure 11-1 Pat and Angie know their pain

"Now, the work we've done lately has been focused on this. Pat is in touch with his fear and Angie is in touch with her shame. Now that you know the pain that you've been running from and defending against all these years, you can share that with your partner. In other words, Pat's prefrontal lobes are going to share his Limbic System's fear with Angie, and Angie's prefrontal lobes are going to share her Limbic System's shame with Pat."

My drawing now looks like this:

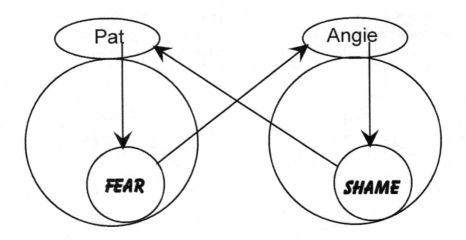

Figure 11-2 Pat and Angie openly share their pain.

The goal is that the adult brain of each of you can look inside the other and see the other's hurt child. During today's session and those that touched on Pat's pain, it was obvious, seeing the response each of you experienced in reaction to the other's pain, that you did that. What was the feeling you felt as you saw each other go through that experience?"

Pat spoke up, "Like I said, I felt bad. I guess I wanted to fix it."

"Right, but what was your first impulse when you realized what she was going through?"

"I wanted to comfort her."

"How about you, Angie? Remember Pat's experience with his Dad in the other session? What was your first impulse?"

"The same. I never realized those feelings were that big."

I add some labels to my drawing and change the arrows.

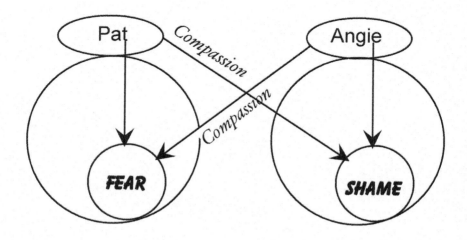

Figure 11-3 My definition of intimacy

"You see, when you each become aware of the other's true feelings, the natural response is compassion. And compassion is the key to intimacy, as we have seen vividly displayed between the two of you. Compassion makes you move toward the other person. The key to compassion is to become vulnerable enough to know about your own pain and to be real enough to share it with your partner. The result is true intimacy."

Chapter 12

The Secret of True Intimacy

The secret of true intimacy is knowing and sharing our pain. Next chapter.

Sorry, I got carried away there. Let's recap a bit to put this little gem in perspective. Everyone leaves childhood with some kind of emotional pain. The pain is a result of emotional needs that were unmet during those first critical relational encounters in childhood. For Unicorns, the need is safety. For Lions, the need is approval. The pain engendered by carrying those unmet needs becomes the central organizing factor of the personality for the rest of a person's life. It is, in fact, the organizing factor behind nearly every moment of our lives.

I've heard that men think about sex every thirty seconds and women think about it every two minutes, or something like that. The same thing is happening with respect to the pain of our unmet emotional needs. At some level our brains drop whatever else they were attending to and attend to this pain every few minutes or so. This process becomes such a second nature to us that we don't notice that we do it.

When people come into my office, they express this pain over and over. We embed it in nearly everything we say. Just yesterday, for example, I had a client who used the words "caged," "trapped," and "controlled" about twenty times in an hour. These picture words are heavily laden with the anxiety and the discomfort that goes with being close. His unconscious was talking to me about his feelings. Meanwhile, he's talking about leaving his marriage. Why? He doesn't want to be caged, trapped, or controlled. What he doesn't understand is that leaving the marriage will not solve the problem. The problem is one that lives inside his mind. His child brain is crying out for freedom, and instead of getting to the bottom of how to get it, he keeps trying to change his circumstances.

The Marriage Contract

So on our wedding day we arrive at the altar with this heavy burden. The subconscious agenda behind the wedding is that this other person will finally heal our pain. Of course, we're completely unaware of our pain and how it drove us to the altar. But we expect our partner to "get it" and heal us nonetheless. They have the same hidden agenda.

"Okay, Sally. I take you to be my lawfully wedded bride, to have and to hold, as long as you prove to be safe and never make any emotional demands on me."

"Ralph, I take you as my husband so that you can give me what my mother never gave me: approval, acceptance, and a sense of importance. Recognition wouldn't be bad either. By the way, I promise never to tell you what I want since I don't know that myself. Your job will be to give me what I want without knowing what it is. If you don't give it to me I will become overwhelmed with pain and blame your ass, scream at you, and eventually divorce you."

"Sounds good to me, Sally, as long as you meet my unmet emotional needs. And by the way, even knowing what they are is far too threatening for me so I won't go there. And if you go there, I'll call you a prying, nagging bitch and run like hell."

And they both say, "'Til death do us part."

The minister smiles and says, "Let the game begin!"

The key to everything is the pain. It drives our thoughts, our lifestyle, our reactions, and our perceptions. Yet we don't know it or notice it. Famed Zen Buddhist monk Thich Nhat Hanh is one teacher who knows about this. He talks about mindfulness and offers meditations to do with one's partner. He might start a meditation, for example, by saying something like, "Darling, I know you are feeling pain." It is extremely helpful and healing to be able to visualize your partner's pain.

The issue I have with some of the followers and proponents of brother Hanh's teaching is that, in order to do the meditation, you have to feel your own pain. It is impossible to empathize with your partner's pain without having some sense of what your own pain feels like. If, like most of us, you are heavily defended and on the run from the hurt inside of you, imagining your partner's pain is just an exercise in repeating words without real feeling.

Know Your Pain

Intimacy is a goal, not a given. Intimacy doesn't arrive in a relationship like a pigeon that homes in on a perch. The first step in achieving intimacy is knowing your pain.

If you can actually *feel* your pain, you may be able to understand someone else's pain. Having access to your pain doesn't mean, though, that you let that part of you take over your life. It simply means that you acknowledge it instead of defending against it.

Knowing your pain means that you honestly admit you are sometimes weak and helpless. It means you know how desperately you want recognition (Lion). It means you are willing to face the full extent of your anxieties (Unicorn).

Why is knowing your pain so important? Because that's where all of the power is. Turning to a defense leaves each of us powerless. The Lion who is acting out anger has no power. Throwing a fit is the single most powerless, most vulnerable thing we can do. Avoiding is also a journey into powerlessness. Disappearance is the ultimate adventure in weakness.

Admitting that I as a Lion am desperate for approval gives me the opportunity to consider the possibility that my partner might be carrying something just as big inside of them.

The other day I was counseling a woman, and asked her to make contact with her loneliness. When she did, she became overwhelmed and had to end the exercise. I explained to her that the feeling, as big as it is, is no bigger than the fear inside her husband. She looked at me with a sudden recognition. She had never considered that something that big might be inside of him, too. And the reason she had never done so was clear in that moment. Since she has been unwilling to see how huge her loneliness is, how could she possibly see the extent of his fear?

We spend so much time and energy not feeling the true authentic emotions that are inside of us. The numbness this requires us to develop incapacitates us when it comes to understanding what goes on with other people.

Another factor that blinds us to our partner's pain is cultural or role stereotypes. It isn't fashionable to see the pain inside of a man; men are supposed to be strong. But just because the pain doesn't show doesn't mean it's not there. How else could a man be afraid to be close? What a ridiculous notion! Lions project strength. That doesn't mean they don't have feelings. Yet if we see someone who is powerful or confident, we wrongly assume that he or she has no needs. Great, I'm off the hook with that person.

How do we find our pain? The best way to do that is through engaging your own autobiographical story. Talking about those things and relationships in your past that left you wanting and hurting leads you to where you need to be. An important aspect of that is feeling your way back into who you were when these things happened. Looking at the pain from an adult point of view is too distant. We must look at it from the viewpoint of the child who lived it.

Long ago, you left behind a little girl or little boy. Filled with fear or shame, that little person took refuge in your unexpressed, unacknowledged feelings. That hurt part of you lives inside. You need to return to your past, to the events that created the hurt, and take care of that part of you. Call it the inner child, if you will. You need to return down the mountain of accomplishment to the little house where it all started, to the tearful child that you left behind.

One thing I often do is to have a client tell their story. Then I ask them to imagine that their own child, their actual living son or daughter, had to live through what they lived through. Can they imagine the pain, the consequences? They can. They are horrified. It's okay that it happened to them, but not to their child. No way!

After all these years, we think there's a nine-hundred-pound gorilla locked up inside, banging at the door. If we let it out, it will destroy us—or at least wreak havoc in our lives. If we would just unlock the door that hides our pain, we would find a little child, grateful that someone finally heard them crying.

When we really know our pain, when we learn to feel the feeling inside that we don't want to feel, when we no longer object to it, we're finally ready for intimacy. We do this by noticing our defensive behavior and then feeling the feeling that drives it.

See Your Partner's Pain

Having reached the point in your own growth that you can fully feel the feelings you would rather defend against, you're now ready to see your partner's pain. Let's be clear about something though: There is no one person who is "sicker" than another in a relationship.

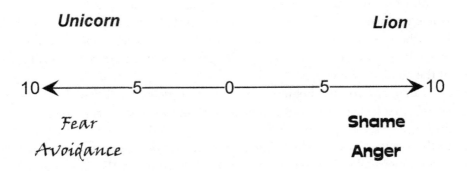

Figure 12-1 We find someone at our level of pain.

If we look at the diagram and assume that on a scale of zero to ten I'm a Lion with a level-five amount of pain and dysfunction, I will manage to find a Unicorn who is a five on the Unicorn scale. Despite appearances to the contrary, we tend to find someone at our own level. We don't stay in relationships with people who are not at our level. So, in looking at our partner's pain, we need to recognize that it is as big as our own. Their adaptive strategies will be in relationship to a degree of dysfunction that matches our own. It is important to realize that the defense is as big as the pain it is defending.

You may appear to be the crazy one or the healthy one in a relationship, but don't kid yourself. You have a big agenda with this other person and that agenda is about you, your pain, your struggle with the pain, and your defense of that pain.

When you look at your partner, imagine the little girl or boy that lives inside of the person. If it helps to superimpose your own child or a child who is close to you to get in touch with your feelings, do so. Once you catch a vision of that exiled, pain-filled child that lives in them, a miracle will happen.

As a couple processes through their personal pain in therapy, it is amazing to see the response of their partner. The impulse is always to move closer. What amazes me is how often, when we get right down to the real nitty-gritty of what happened in childhood, the other person is hearing their partner's story for the first time. There may be horrendous stories of abuse, or just the disappointment of daily family life, but it is shocking how little of this information has ever made its way into the marriage. It is not unusual at all, as the story unfolds, to see the spouse's jaw drop in shock and disbelief. They turn to me and say, "I never knew."

Once this happens, two changes occur. First, each person never looks at their partner in the same way. They can see the pain inside the other clearly. The second change is just as dramatic. They want to move closer, to hold or to comfort the other person. That's when I introduce the "Conflict Equation" and the "Healing Equation." They go like this:

The Conflict Equation
Pain + Defense = A Counterattack

In other words, when we defend our pain with anger or avoidance it always looks like an attack to the other person. So they respond with a counterattack. The Healing Equation goes like this:

The Healing Equation
Pain – Defense =
A Compassionate Response

When you're willing to express your pain in an authentic way without defending, you open the possibility for a compassionate response. And nine times out of ten, you *will* get a compassionate response. Sometimes you don't, or at least not right away.

Most of the time when my clients see this level of what's going on, they freak out. Their reaction is that entering into it as I'm suggesting will never work. I agree with them that the process does look daunting. But in practice, it's the only thing that works. Defending never works.

We'll explore later how to put this insight into practice. For now, the point to hold on to is that expressing your pain in an authentic way draws out the compassion in the other person. Defending elicits their warrior.

Compassion: the Key to Intimacy

When we feel compassion, we automatically want to move closer to the person who is in pain. When compassion emerges we empathize, we walk a mile in the other person's shoes. But let's get something straight about what compassion is. It's not icky gooey, simpering, whimpering, victimy, sticky stuff. In fact, tough love comes from compassion. I may be the toughest on someone when I'm feeling the most compassionate. That's not to say that experiencing someone's compassion shouldn't be soft and comforting as well. But it is not a fake display of caring.

The ability to be compassionate is one of the qualities that distinguish us from other mammals. Yet we live in a society that teaches that compassion is weakness, especially with regard to men. As a result, we raise many boys and some girls who are nothing more than primates.

Intimacy means close, personal contact. It means understanding, validation, and familiarity. If we don't know our partner's pain, we don't know *them*; intimacy is not possible. When we do know their pain, compassion leads us to intimacy.

The Ultimate Payoff

There are several payoffs for all this hard work of developing awareness. We finally get a fulfilling relationship. Our unmet emotional needs get met. And there's no more mystery about how to satisfy our partner.

Once our pain is out in the open, we can finally ask for and get what we want in the relationship. If we've been yearning for approval, recognition, acceptance, importance, a sense of equality, specialness, or closeness, we can now ask for it and our motivation will be clear. If we want closeness without the pressure and discomfort that comes from taking responsibility for the other person's happiness, we can ask for it. If we want to feel safe and close at the same time, it will make sense. If we fear failure and want support, if we're jealous and want reassurance, if we're intimidated or overwhelmed and want space, we can request it. Suddenly things make sense.

Living with someone who knows you and finally understands where you're coming from is my definition of fulfillment. The relationship becomes a haven, an escape, a place to recharge. You want to come home.

One of the biggest problems that Unicorns have is the challenge of satisfying their partner. Since they look through a lens of fear, it looks like they must negotiate a "honey do" list for themselves a mile long to fulfill their partner.

A simple thing like taking out the garbage can become the most enormous burden in the world. Just thinking about it can bring up stultifying resistance. However, when seen through the framework of the Lion's shame, taking out the garbage shrinks to insignificance as compared to the emotional payoff the Lion gets out of doing it. If I can make my partner's day by simply taking out the garbage, I'm going to do it.

The shoe also fits on the other foot. Lion Harmon used to greet his Unicorn wife at the door and dump all the stress of his day on her. He wanted her to be close and make him feel better. After learning what goes through the mind of a Unicorn, he learned to signal that he was safe to be with by giving her a quick kiss and a smile before retreating to another part of the house. When she felt comfortable, she would follow him and ask about his day. Giving her that space and the reassurance that she was not the focus of a conflict was all she needed to settle into nesting with him, as opposed to girding herself for an evening of challenge and appeasement.

Another payoff of getting the process of intimacy right is that you find that it doesn't take long to fulfill your partner's unmet emotional needs. Taking out the garbage takes only a couple of minutes, but the signal it sends emotionally is immense. Yielding space takes little real effort, but the payoff in responsiveness is huge. It takes so little to change the dynamic between couples. When you roll over in bed in the morning simply ask yourself, "What does this little girl or little boy next to me need today?" Give it to them freely and without reservation, and your life will change forever.

Chapter 13

A Model for Change

The Brutishness of Unconsciousness

Wilder is gesturing vehemently at a stack of books and papers he just plopped on the coffee table. He's somewhat burly, with violent eyebrows and a dark face. "Heinrich von Widdle wrote three chapters in this book," he nearly shouts. "Here are a number of journal articles, too. He postulates that her fear of intimacy could be a head injury. Granted, it's rare, but not uncommon."

I look at his wife, Emily. She is a slight woman whose dark hair highlights her ivory skin. Her hair looks a little disheveled or poorly trimmed. I can't tell which. Her eyes are wide and she has become completely still. She has gone into freeze mode.

I clear my voice, trying to show some interest in what Wilder is saying, "I'm not sure I understand what you mean. Obviously, you think she has this rare condition."

Wilder grabs one of the many papers in the stack. "Right here is a case study very similar to Emily. Of course, this woman was hit in the head with a shopping cart instead of garbage cans."

I look to Emily, who is becoming paler by the moment. "You got hit in the head with a garbage can?"

"A number of years ago we had a freak storm, and early one morning there was some black ice on the road. When I took out the garbage, I fell and all of the cans came down on me. The doctor said I had a mild concussion."

"Right," interjects Wilder, "and von Widdle says that those are the exact conditions that can set up the syndrome."

"Okay," I say, "let me kind of recap here just so I understand the situation. Wilder, you think that the reason that Emily wants a divorce and is so afraid to be close to you is because she has von Widdle's syndrome due to the unfortunate business with the garbage cans."

"Right."

"And Emily, tell me what your perspective is on all of this."

She looks to be gathering strength for a moment and then says, "I came from an extremely abusive background. My therapist says I rushed into this marriage because I always am a victim wanting to be rescued. Wilder and I were friends and I just let myself get carried away. Now I need my space. I'm just tired of being afraid so I have to get a divorce. My therapist says I still need more time to recover."

"And how long, may I ask, have you been seeing this therapist?"

"About three and a half years."

At this point Wilder jumps in. "I've told Emily that that is just sick dependency. Her therapist has poisoned her mind."

"Emily, how do you feel when Wilder talks like that?"

"I feel frightened. I just freeze with terror. I don't know what to do."

"Does it ever offend you that Wilder has diagnosed you and judged your relationship with your therapist?"

"Of course. I feel belittled and unimportant."

Yep, I think to myself, she has been in therapy all right. This situation is hopeless. Emily has made her decision.

"Emily," I ask, "I'm curious. If you're so intent on a divorce, why drive forty-five miles to see me?"

"I told Wilder I would do it. I'm here to support him."

"And Wilder, your intention in being here?"

"I was hoping that you could help me convince her to seek medical help before she files for divorce."

I chuckle openly. "I'm afraid you've mistaken me for something I'm not. I don't take sides. One or the other of you can't recruit me. I'm not interested in your fascinating stories about the other person. I'm here to save lives. What I'm hearing is that neither one of you is interested in my services."

"Tell us what to do, Doc," says Wilder.

"I won't tell you what to do. But I will give you my opinion, if you'll listen."

They both nod their heads, so I prepare to give them the only shot I have, which I'm sure will make no difference now. But possibly it will plant a seed for growth in the future.

"Wilder, I'll start with you. Whether or not von Widdle has anything to do with this is beside the point. Emily doesn't want to stay with you. Every time you bring up this syndrome stuff, you look like a maniac. You need to get in touch with the pain that's underneath your acting like that. You're driving her away from you. The unfortunate thing about this is that I know that I'll never see you again, because you don't think you have any responsibility here. You've conveniently sidestepped that with this von Widdle stuff. This simple fact is that you must have enormous pain that you're not dealing with because of what's about to happen. I'm telling you that the pain is the best asset you have. You have to let her go. That's the only thing you can do. That's the only hope you have. As long as she can focus on your desperate attempts to hang on, you give her cover so that she doesn't need to look at what she's doing."

He grunts a noncommittal grunt and I turn to Emily.

"Emily, you're not going to like what I'm about to say. I don't care what your issues are or whether or not getting married was a mistake. The simple fact is that you did get married. As a result, you have an obligation to solve the problem from within that marriage. You do not have the luxury of running and avoiding as ways to solve your problem. What you are doing is extremely cruel and irresponsible. Your therapist's advice is absolutely wrong in my opinion. The best place for you to finish dealing with your hurtful past is right inside a relationship that continually reminds you of it. What you are doing is an act of violence."

A few minutes later, they leave my office. I know I'll never hear from them again. Somehow, I have to let that go. I can't do it for them. They have to want it for themselves more than I want it for them.

Accepting What Is

Pat and Angie literally *bound* into my office. They look like cats with small creatures hidden in their mouths.

"We did it," says Angie.

"Yep," chimes in Pat.

"Did what?"

Angie answers, "Well, we had an argument. The next day we were able to sit down and process through the argument the way you've taught us to do."

"Tell me about it. Give me the details."

Pat and Angie look at one another, trying to decide who is going to tell the story. In classic extraverted Lion fashion, Angie goes ahead.

"Well, I had asked Pat to install a new toilet paper holder in our bathroom. We had gone to the hardware store, picked one out, and brought it home. This was about a month ago. It sat on the counter in the bathroom for about a week, and I finally asked Pat when he was going to install it."

Pat pipes up, "When she asked me that, I could feel myself getting resentful."

He nods for Angie to go ahead. "Anyway, he kind of whined at me that he would get around to it. I got sort of angry, but I decided to let it go. A week went by and I asked him again and got the same response. By then I could tell I was starting to take this really personally. I could tell I was getting angry. Finally, after our last session, I got up on a Saturday determined that he was going to install the damn thing no matter what."

Pat interjects, "And I was equally determined not to let her tell me what to do."

Angie chuckles and goes on. "So we had a big argument about it. I said things that I regret, and he was angry, too. But he did finally install the toilet paper thingamajig. A few hours later I got to thinking about our sessions and what you've been teaching us. I approached Pat about trying to do this a different way. So we got a big piece of paper and laid out the perception–feelings–defensive behavior thing. It took us a few minutes to fill out each piece of it."

Pat interrupts at this point. "It was all right there. Angie could see how she was taking it all personally and how it made her feel unimportant, like her father didn't care about her. And I suddenly got this flash that what I was doing was resisting my father. The whole time I had been passively punishing Angie, thinking, 'She can't tell me what to do.' But when we laid it out on paper, I realized this was all about my Dad. I could see how much it was hurting Angie."

"Anyway, we made up and had a wonderful weekend," concluded Angie, followed by an embarrassing silence, during which they remembered Saturday night and I sat looking blank and innocent.

Finally, I speak up. "You guys really see it, don't you? I can't tell you how gratified I am. Hearing you makes it all worthwhile for me."

"We just have one question," states Pat. "Now that we know all this, what would have been a better way to have handled the situation?"

"First of all, the most powerful tool you have is the awareness of what's going on inside of you. For you, Pat, that's going to be this fear, this discomfort. You must see yourself trying to escape. When you get resentful, you know you're starting to feel trapped.

"And for you, Angie, you need to see the anger come up and immediately tell yourself that this is about the pain of not feeling cared for, not being special. So awareness of your personal process is essential. The next thing is to notice that the other person's behavior is about their pain and their process of how to defend against that pain. Although we're seemingly talking about a toilet paper holder, actually we're talking about a huge emotional thing you both carry around inside of you. Embedded in the smallest disagreement is the universe of who you are because of your pain and defenses."

"Yes, but what do we *do*?" asks Angie. "Let's say that I use my awareness and I see what's happening. Then what?"

"Let me introduce you to what I call *acceptance*."

Pat and Angie give me a quizzical look.

"Remember we talked about the conflict equation and the healing equation?"

They both nod.

"The key to getting a compassionate response when thinking about those principles is to express the pain honestly, right? Now you know what the pain is. The pain is the feeling that's driving the defense. It may be fear, it may be feeling trapped or suffocated; it may be shame, a feeling like nobody cares; it may be loneliness, abandonment—whatever. But no matter what it is, the key to getting your partner to respond compassionately is to state the feeling with no defense at all. This may seem like it leaves you too vulnerable; but actually, it's very powerful.

What we're going to do is to use *acceptance* to accomplish this. I'm going to completely accept your behavior for what it is: your behavior. And I'm not going to ask you to change your behavior. That's step one.

Step two is I'm going to take complete responsibility for my feeling and reaction. If I'm feeling hurt, shamed, or like nobody cares, that's about me. It's not my partner's responsibility. I know that feelings are a result of my perception and not of my partner's behavior, and I'm going to take responsibility for that.

This leads to step three. I'm going to ask my partner for help with my feeling."

I write the steps on the board.

Step 1: Acceptance
Step 2: Taking responsibility
Step 3: Asking for what I truly want

"So here's the template," I say as I write on the board:

> *The problem is not your behavior. The problem is my reaction to your behavior, which comes from my feeling. Will you help me with my feeling?*

Pat and Angie are looking at me as if I've lost my mind. I turn to them and say, "Let me give you an example. Let's go back to the toilet thingamabob. It has been going on for a week now and I'm Angie and I'm starting to get angry about it. Using this template, I'm going to accept that Pat can install it or not install it. It's really his choice what he decides to do. So I'm not going to try and change his behavior.

"However, since I'm getting angry I know that it's because I feel he doesn't care about me. So I'm going to take responsibility for that feeling. In other words, that feeling is about me, Angie, not about Pat.

"Next, I'm going to ask Pat for help with my feeling.

"So here goes. Angie, you would say something like this: 'Pat I noticed that you haven't installed the toilet thingy yet. When I see it lying on the counter, I get this feeling that you don't care about me. I know that's not true. Can you help me with my feeling that you don't care about me?'"

Angie burst out. "Oh, sure, I'm going to do that! He'll just tell me tough luck."

"Wait a minute Angie," I say. "Let's see. Pat, if she said that to you, what would your immediate response be?"

"I would want to know how I could help her feel loved."

Angie looks stunned. We run through the principles for a few minutes and rehearse a little. Then I send them on their way.

Chapter 14

Accepting Responsibility and Asking for Help

The day I was finishing the previous chapter, a new couple came into my office for counseling. Every time she said anything that contained the word "you," he would have an emotional reaction. I said to him, "Let's do a little experiment."

I looked him right in the eye and said, "*You* are the problem in this relationship."

He immediately started to defend himself and blame her.

I tried it again, emphasizing that this was an exercise and his job was to watch what happened inside him. Again, as soon as I said anything that sounded like blaming him, he would become defensive and start blaming her. We talked about it, and I tried it repeatedly. Soon it became apparent, even to him, that his mind was so conditioned that he couldn't pull himself out of his emotions long enough to understand what is really going on around him.

Of course, this is the situation for all of us to some extent. We're continually distorting, remembering and associating, making value judgments, spouting our point of view and philosophies, and being overwhelmed with emotions. This process is so automatic that we don't notice it at all. We literally live in a house of mirrors where reality bends and distorts itself around our survival needs and instincts. We don't ever question it. Tragically, we rarely ever see reality for what it is.

If we are Lions, we see it all as personal. We live in a world that's trying to dump on us at any moment. Nobody loves us, nobody cares, and life is a struggle for recognition and acceptance. If we're Unicorns, we see the world as a wildly spinning planet. We must hold on tight before we spin off, careening into uncharted space. People around us live chaotic, threatening lives. Their emotions are overwhelming to us. These people are out of control. For us, life is an unending series of open-field dashes to find peace and safe haven.

Accepting Responsibility

To find our way out of this house of mirrors, we must accept that how we behave is a function of our feelings. Feelings arise from "perceptions" that support the instinctive view of reality we developed way back, based on our earliest survival needs. Until we realize that our reactions are about *us,* and that they tell us *nothing* about anyone else, we will never go free.

Accepting responsibility, then, is the first step. If our marriage is not working, it's our responsibility. If life isn't working, the finger of blame points back to us. If we're unhappy and unfulfilled, it's about us and no one else. Our perceived world reflects the world our childhood constructed inside of us. We can't change the exterior world and expect the interior world to change. It's the other way around. We need internal inspection. If we see everything as an attack, we need to check our glasses.

So the question becomes not, "Oh God, why is this happening to me?" but "Oh God, show me what this means about me." Embedded in every reaction and every conflict—in every situation—is something that we can learn about ourselves: who we are and what we're up to. We all have a hidden emotional agenda, and until we bring it out clearly and see it, we will never discover why our life isn't working.

Accepting responsibility is number one.

Without Awareness There Is No Choice

Each of us carries an emotional process inside of us. It follows the pattern of perceptions, which drive emotions, which drive behavior. Emotions drive behavior. This comes as quite a shock to many of my clients when they start therapy. They are convinced that they "just get angry." No one just gets angry. Shame drives anger. Fear drives avoidance.

Our emotional process has two qualities that make it ultimately easy to understand and identify. First, it's always the same. This cycling from perception to feeling to behavior is the same. The pattern is constant and is repeated over and over. Second, the feeling that we don't want to feel is always the same feeling. In the car, in the house, at work, with our spouse, with our kids—it doesn't matter. Our emotional process remains constant. When our button gets pushed, our perceptions, feelings, and behaviors are predictable and consistent.

What is essential is for us to become aware of our own internal process. And what's funny about this is that when people learn how their process works, they immediately say, "Okay, so what do I do? How do I change my behavior?" When I tell them, they look at me as if I'm crazy. The answer is *awareness*. Most of us confuse understanding with awareness.

Understanding means we get it. We know the concept. It makes sense. We can repeat it. We can remember it. Awareness is nothing like that. *Awareness is the process of forcing ourselves out of full association with our experience in order to watch ourselves experience it. Awareness, in other words, is that knowledge we gain through self-observation. It differs from understanding, which is knowledge we gain through observations of the world around us.*

Self-Observation

We are the only species on earth that can engage in self-observation and articulate what we see. Well, I should qualify that a little. Certain types of high primates do appear to have the power of self-observation, but without anything we recognize as verbal speech. Some gorillas, for example, have been trained to talk in sign language, and their use of it does give the appearance that they have the capacity for self-referencing.

In any event, the ability to self-observe takes place in the prefrontal lobes of the cerebral cortex or neo-cortex. "Neo" means "new," as in the new brain. The new brain has the ability to observe itself. We can literally watch our brain's process and make comments about the process we are noticing. It is the process of mind minding the mind.

Meditation is helpful in training self-observation. The idea behind *vispassana* or insight meditation is to calm the mind, and begin to watch thoughts bubbling up out of the mind, and to let them go without attaching any significance to them. I am a firm believer that insight meditation is a

127

powerful tool in taking control back from the Limbic System. It produces true liberation.

Observing yourself in the act of life itself is also powerful. Formal sit-down meditation is challenging, but watching your thoughts as you are up and about the act of living is even more challenging. Another word for this is *mindfulness*. Again, this is the mind watching itself.

What I do in my work with couples is even simpler. I train them to watch their reactions. If you are a Lion, I want you to become fully aware of your anger. I want you to watch it rise and fall, come and go. I want you to become a master of observing your own anger.

Unicorns must become aware of their avoidance. Watch yourself escape. See yourself shut down. Watch the door of your heart slam shut. Earn a Master's degree in how you defend yourself by fleeing.

After all, the parts that defend us are valuable resources. We don't want to despise our anger or ignore the voice of our protector. Ultimately, we may opt for a different strategy, but we do not want to disown these parts of us.

I can hear many readers saying, "I don't want to own my anger. Yuk!"

The problem is that *what we won't own owns us*. The more we ignore, stuff, shut down, run from, or deny the darkness inside of us, the more power we give it. By bringing it out into the light and embracing it, we become whole and integrated, ready once again to exercise choice in our lives. Self-observation lets us do that.

Only after we have thoroughly understood our defenses can we probe the next level—the feelings that underlie the defenses. We become aware of them through direct observation also.

By the time we're ready to look into those feelings we have a powerful tool: being alert to when our defenses kick in. When we know we have just had a defensive and emotional reaction, we also know we have just defended ourselves against a feeling we don't want to feel. Even if we can't *feel* the feeling, studying our defense provides a map to where the feeling is. Self-observation is again the tool to use. Our adult brain observes our child brain and ferrets out the hidden emotion from the pain we carry deep in our hearts.

If you are a Unicorn, for example, know you're looking for something that feels like fear, anxiety, nervousness, pressure, discomfort. If you're a Lion, the feeling you're looking for is a feeling of being unacceptable, unloved, discounted, disregarded, disrespected, not cared for. Take these two templates and go look for the feeling.

Once you firmly understand and feel the feeling, you're ready for the final frontier: your perceptions. You must ask the question, "What do I perceive is happening?" Even if reality and perception actually match up in this case, you now have a range of options. Automatic process dictates only one response, flight or fight. Awareness gives us real choice.

Acceptance

So let's say we're at the point where you have accepted responsibility that your feelings and reactions belong to and are generated by you. You might still be inclined to protest on occasion and say, "But, she pushed my button." Trust me; she doesn't know where your button is. It's in your head. Your button is your responsibility.

You've exercised some awareness of your own emotional process. You automatically look deeply inside of yourself and see your reaction as a defense. You notice your pain just underneath the defense and you automatically question your perception of what is happening.

Now you're ready to see your partner for who he or she really is. She isn't running. He isn't attacking. They are people crying out in pain. Anger is a cry for help. Avoidance is a plea for mercy. Inside your partner is a damaged, estranged child who brings a crucible of emotional need to the marriage. You need to be able to see their defense as a defense, not an attack. Lions learn that the partner's is not personal. Unicorns learn to see beyond their partner's anger to the pain underneath it.

The behavior may even be alcoholism or some other dangerous addiction. Let's not sugarcoat this. When we act out our defenses, all hell breaks loose. Destroying furniture is not out of the question.

So what's the problem? If we see our partner's behavior as unacceptable, we're going to pontificate about it. "Smoking is dangerous." "Nobody likes anger." "Some things are just not right." "Pornography is morally wrong." "The Bible says women should submit to men, so you need to be the way I want you to be." No one in the History of Relationship has changed dramatically because of this kind of moralistic nonsense. No one cares about your opinion on how the rest of the world should behave. That opinion will compel no one to change his or her life. Let it go. Self-righteousness is like a rope pulled across a country road. All it does is snarl traffic.

What we're left with when we set aside our precious point of view is acceptance. If our partner is angry, we accept it. If they are avoidant, we accept it. It is what it is, a behavior. It may be an unpleasant behavior, but labeling it will get you nothing but a counterattack.

Reframing the Problem

What does *reframing* mean? When you reframe something, you look at in a different way. You redefine it. You put it in a new context. So if we're going to embrace the concept of acceptance, then the problem cannot be defined as the other person's behavior. With what does that leave us? Our reaction—that's all that's left. So the reframe becomes: The problem isn't your behavior; the problem is my reaction to it.

Oh, boy! I've done it now.

"Girlfriend, he just blamed us for those drinkin', womanizin' men."

"I heard him, sister."

Now wait a minute. Isn't the real problem how you feel inside after all? If you were truly, serenely happy, would you care if he went off with his buddies for some brew? Of course not.

The problem is your reaction. Now concentrate for a minute. Embedded in your reaction is your pain. The feeling you don't want to feel. The problem is that feeling. So reframing the problem must also include your pain.

It goes something like this:

"The problem isn't your behavior; it's my feelings of not being good enough."

Or:

"The problem isn't your behavior, it's my feeling overwhelmed."

Or:

"The problem isn't your behavior, it's my feeling rejected, lonely, afraid, intimidated, unloved, etc., etc., etc."

Your Pain Is Your Power

What I'm pointing to here is the unresolved issues that you have been carrying around inside of you all of your life. If you're a Lion, it has to do with shame. If you're a Unicorn, it has to do with fear.

Looking to your own inner state, rather than to the other person's behavior, sets up the possibility of getting your underlying emotional need met. For Unicorns, this has to do with safety. For Lions, it's about approval in some form or another. Being able to state the pain clearly, without any defense, is essential in order not to trigger the other person's defense. You want the possibility of a compassionate response.

The entire concept goes like this:

"The problem is not your behavior. It's my reaction. When I react, I'm feeling pain. Will you help me with my feeling?"

Take the example of a Unicorn dealing with a Lion's anger. It would go something like this: "When I see you so angry, I feel frightened and unsafe. It makes me want to run away. But I really want to be with you and not run away. Will you help me feel safer?"

Or a Lion dealing with the avoidance of the Unicorn: "When you don't respond to me, I feel rejected. Please help me with my feelings of rejection."

There are two important things to understand about this procedure. First, you must never try it when the other person is already triggered. You will not get a compassionate response if you try it at that time. Second, there is no guarantee of success in using this technique. All it does is to open up space for the other person to make a different choice. There is one guarantee, however: If you don't try this, if you use a defense instead, you will reinforce the circular, recursive problem.

Success in this process requires several things that may appear risky. You must know your pain and be able to talk about it openly with your partner. When I first introduce this, some people are horrified that it will leave them too vulnerable. Actually, hiding the pain is what makes us most vulnerable. In addition, if you're in a relationship with someone with whom you are truly afraid to become vulnerable, it might be time to reassess your choice of partner.

I get a lot of flack when I introduce this approach. What is more important, however, is that it often results in a miracle response. Many times the response is not only compassionate and nurturing, but the partner will say something like, "I never knew you felt that way. I don't want you to feel that way."

Quite literally, when we defend, we become powerless. When we allow ourselves to become aware of our pain and are open about it, we become far more powerful.

Hidden in this approach is the implication that I am taking responsibility for my pain, my emotional needs, and myself. In psychology, we call this "differentiation of self." This means that I am an independent person, I am not dependent on you, and I am taking charge of getting my emotional needs met.

This attitude breaks the relationship out of its self-reflexive system and signals that the game-playing is over. At least one person has decided to be a grown-up.

Chapter 15

The Exercise of Personal Power

Resisting Authority and Serving God

Chad is sitting in the chair. Looking at me. He has read a draft of my book (this book) about the Lion and Unicorn concept. I gave it to him with the hope that he would read it and have a breakthrough. He thinks there is enormous sales potential for the book and wants to help me market it.

"I just think it would help a countless number of people. And let's face it, I want to help people, but I also want the money. If I can help you and make some serious money at the same time, great!"

"Just why do you think the book is so good?"

"The concept is very simple. You've boiled it down to just two types. Some of those others have a lot of bullshit—three types, ten types. This is simple enough for people to understand."

I look at him. Chad is a Unicorn raised by a patriarchal father who issued orders for everything, and hardly let him breathe without permission. Being a Unicorn, he wants to run,. But when Unicorns get trapped, they push back. When they feel trapped for a long period, a tremendous internal resistance and rebellion builds up inside of them. Now, decades later, here he sits. The world looks like a large family with everyone telling him what to do.

"I appreciate the compliment on my work, but I'm asking you what it means to you personally. What did you learn as you read it?"

"You know, it's interesting. I can see more where people are coming from now. Their bullshit is a lot more apparent to me. It makes me think of what I really want to do with my life. I don't want to sound religious, but I just want to serve God."

I lean forward and ask, "When you say other people's bullshit, what do you mean?"

"It's all a game. They're all acting out their stuff. It's all manipulation. It's about control. They're just trying to force their own stuff down your throat and my throat."

"Chad, focus on my question for a moment. I understand what you're saying. But I want to know what the book meant to you personally."

"Personally? It feels pretty scary. I got this far in life without too much trouble. I guess I don't want to let that go. I mean, I may be all screwed up, but whatever I'm doing must be somewhat okay. I'm able to operate my own small business. I don't have a boss telling me what to do or dictating to me. I come and go as I please. I make a reasonable living. I'm having a hard time seeing what the problem is."

I chuckle. "Let me tell you what the problem is. Sprinkled throughout what you've been telling me are words like 'trapped' and phrases like 'forcing down my throat' and 'nobody is going to tell me what to do.'"

I add, "Let's try an exercise. I'll say something and you tell me the first thing that goes through your mind."

"Okay."

"Now listen carefully. Don't think of purple cows." I let a moment pass and then ask, "What was the first thing that went through your mind?"

He grins at me broadly. "Why, a purple cow, of course."

"Your father dictated to you. He told you what to do and when to do it. He wouldn't let you breathe your own air. This set up an enormous resistance in you to the point that every thought you think is against the backdrop of your determination not to let your father tell you what to do. Your mind is so conditioned that everything you say contains the predicate of that resistance. It's embedded in every message, in every thought, in every comment that you produce."

Chad is looking at me blankly.

"Chad, what do you think I'm doing right now?"

"I guess, if I were to be honest, I'd say you're just another guy trying to tell me what to do."

"You said you ultimately want to serve God. I want to tell you what I really, really am. I'm God—because God is inside of all of us—and I'm asking you to come and be free, and be here with me, where I am. But you can't hear me because everything you hear comes through the filter of 'I have to resist authority figures.' What do you think of that?"

"I have a little problem with the 'God' part."

Avoiding the Train Wreck

"I don't know what to do, Dude."

Armando's wife is leaving him after twelve years of his being emotionally unavailable and drunk. He is overwrought. Fortunately, he saw right away that he is a Unicorn and that fear has driven his behavior. Unfortunately, it may be too late.

"Should I ask her out on a date?"

"Go ahead, but be prepared. She'll probably punish you in the process."

"What do you mean?"

"She's angry at you. She'll probably jerk you around a little."

"Oh, she does that! She'll say, 'I'll let you know' or 'if I have the time.'"

"That's what I mean."

"Yeah, Dude. What am I supposed to do? Should I ask her for sex?"

I chuckle. "No, Armando, don't ask her for sex. Ask her to come over for dinner. When she arrives, have a nice meal prepared. Buy a $30 bottle of wine. Light some candles."

"Romance."

"Right."

"Dude, we made love last week. I did everything for her."

"Great. If you get another chance, do the same thing. Remember the biggest erogenous zone on a woman."

"What's an erogenous zone?"

"An area that turns her on."

"Oh, I gotchya."

"So what/s the biggest erogenous zone for a woman?"

"I don't know, Dude."

I reach up and point to my head, touching my finger above the eye.

Armando looks surprised. "I'm supposed to kiss her forehead?"

Enlightened Ignorance

"Oh my God!" exclaims Angie. "I'm telling you, I could *see* it. There it was in black and white. I had been meditating on my anger and the shame that's underneath the anger. I had been praying for days for some higher power to show me the source of it all. I was thinking about my father and my little brother. One day, when I was in the park taking my lunch break, across the lawn I heard a mother scolding her little girl and suddenly I remembered."

"What did you remember?"

"One day my little brother and I were out playing. Since I was two years older than he was, it was my job to watch him. We were playing on a slide at the park. We decided it would be fun to go up the slide backwards. A few of the children started up the slide from the bottom. The slide was slippery, and the girl in front of my brother suddenly lost her footing and her foot flew out, kicking him in the face. Blood started to pour out of his mouth. When I got home, my father went into a tirade. It was my fault, he claimed. My brother ended up having a crown put on one of his teeth. I felt responsible for that."

"How old were you at the time?" I ask.

"I was eight and my brother was six. I think that tooth was his first permanent molar."

"Anyway, as I was remembering that, I remembered an even earlier incident. When I was five and my brother was three, he took a crayon and drew stuff on the wall of his room. My Dad went into a rage when he found out. When I heard what was happening, I ran up to my brother's room and cried out, 'Dad, don't hit him. He's just a little kid. Hit me instead.'"

"Well, he broke into a broad smile and said what a good little girl I was. Guess who ended up cleaning the walls? Me."

Pat is looking at her in admiration. He knows that Angie has had an epiphany. He's not sure what it is, but he knows that it's very important.

Angie isn't done. Her voice is excited as if she has just discovered the fountain of youth—or, more accurately, the true meaning of life.

"Now I understand what the pattern is. Now I see. I've been this way my whole life! I had to take responsibility for everyone else's feelings and fix them. If I didn't, it meant I wasn't good enough. I can't articulate everything I'm seeing right now. Do I sound crazy?"

136

I clear my voice so as not to sound too choked up. "Angie, I understand exactly what you're saying. You're standing outside of yourself and looking in. You see who you are and how your conditioning has defined your life. This is nothing short of a rebirth. It's only the beginning. Welcome to the new world!"

Pat finally interjects. "I know what happened for Angie has changed her life forever. I can see how big it is. These last few days have been like living with a new woman."

Angie is still excited. When Pat and Angie first came into my office, they both were unaware of their ignorance. They were defending, attacking, and feeling enormous hurt. They thought they knew all the answers.

Angie has suddenly entered into a new dimension of knowing. She knows that she doesn't know. She has been enlightened to her ignorance. She can see how unawareness has exacted a toll in her life. She is like a little child, a newborn, ready to enter a new world of learning and experience through the lens of pure awareness.

Equipped by the awareness of her ignorance, she can enter into and share in the pure divinity of each moment of life, and experience it fully. In his book, *The Contemplative Heart*, James Finley sums this up: "The more we become consciously present to our difficulty in being consciously present, the more present the difficulty becomes."

By knowing that she doesn't know, Angie can watch her own cycling of unawareness and know that the ebb and flow of awareness takes her in and out of the full-time presence of the divinity of life. She can watch herself alternate between the glory of pure existence and being, and the pallor of utter darkness and separation. Being both humbled and fulfilled in her awareness of her ignorance, she has the opportunity to use her ignorance as a powerful tool to drive her awareness toward the light that gives birth to each moment. She achieves this by contemplating the depths of her ignorance, by seeing the sleep that she sleeps and the drugs of early learning, conditioning, and adapting that caused that sleep.

I look at Pat. He hasn't made the transition in himself to where she is. He still doesn't know that he doesn't know. He thinks he knows. But what he knows is only what his fear and rage, in addition to his strivings, will let him know. Angie, in sharp contrast, is enlightened to that ignorance in herself, and refuses to play the "I know" game anymore.

I become aware of my own ignorance as well as I interact with Pat and Angie. I have found that unless I'm willing to sit in the crucible of my own rage, pain, and alienation, I experience no awareness. I watch my needs and reactions vie for control of my mind; and as I let compassion for my own unawareness flow through me, my eyes too, are opened. I can't run from my ignorance and I can't hide from my pain. If I do, I hide from myself, and I close up. Awareness vanishes, and along with it any chance of helping them.

While I've been musing, Angie's fervor has dissipated somewhat. Pat has lapsed into questions about Angie's anger. I realize that I'm still going to have to give solid emotional tools to help both of them. Epiphanies are one thing, but we still must mow the lawn.

"I want to talk to you for a moment," I resume, "about a concept called 'validation.' And after I explain it, we'll tie it in to what we talked about last week."

Pat and Angie shift in their chairs, ready to listen.

"Let's assume for a moment that when you come home, Pat, Angie is angry because you forgot to take out the garbage that morning. You notice that your first impulse is to run, avoid, or shut down emotionally. Instead of doing that, you validate her. Now, before I tell you what validation *is*, I want you to understand what validation is not.

"Validation is *not* giving the other person permission to stay angry, or to continue some other defensive behavior. Also, validation is *not* agreeing with the other person's point of view. So, validation isn't permission and it isn't agreement. It *is* awareness, and it goes like this. Using our example of the garbage, Pat, what would Angie be saying to you?"

Pat thinks for a moment and then the light goes on. "She would be saying that I don't care about her. That's what she always says, because that's how her father treated her."

"Great, Pat, that's a huge insight. So here's what you say. 'If you had promised to take out the garbage for me and hadn't done it, I might have felt the same way.' Now what's interesting about this?"

I see Angie with a broad smile on her face.

"Okay, say it," I tell her.

"It just felt so good. I thought, 'Finally, someone understands!'"

"Pat, Angie just made the point far more forcefully than I could have. What validation says to the other person is, 'If I were in your shoes I would feel those feelings, too.' What this signals to the other person is that you really understand their pain. That's all they want. They don't want excuses

138

or explanations, and they don't want the incident minimized or trivialized. They want to know that you truly understand the feeling that they feel.

So what you're going to say is something like this: 'If I thought that was happening to me, I'd be angry too.' You're saying that given your perception, distorted or not, you have a right to your anger. We're not saying, 'You have a right to act out your anger.'

"On the other hand, when you are likely to avoid, Angie might say something like: 'If I thought I was with a real scary person, I would avoid, too.'"

Pat looks thoughtful. "I get it. I really do. But what do I do with my fear then?"

"Aw, that's a great question. It takes us back to last week's session." I go to the board and start to write. "You remember that there were basically three steps to what we learned last week, right? Do you both remember the first step?"

"Acceptance," pipes up Angie.

"Right. First accept the other person's behavior. What's next?"

Pat thinks for a second and says, "Responsibility?"

"Right. Then, finally, we ask for what we want in terms of our emotional needs. Today, though, we'll add validation as our new first step. It goes like this:

VALIDATION
ACCEPTANCE
RESPONSIBILITY
ASKING FOR OUR NEEDS TO BE MET

"So, first we *validate* the other person's feelings. We basically say, 'You have a right to your feelings and, given your perception, your feelings makes sense.' Then we *accept* the other person's defensive behavior. Third, we take *responsibility* for our reactions and feelings and say that they are about us. Finally, we ask our partner for help with our feelings and the emotional needs that go with them."

"So here's what it would sound like for Angie talking about Pat. Let's say Pat arrives home late and doesn't call Angie because he's afraid of her anger. Angie might say, 'Pat, I understand that you need to stay late sometimes and that it's difficult to call because you think I might be angry and you don't want to experience conflict. You have a right not to call if you're anxious about my reaction. When you don't call, though, I feel that you don't care about me. I know that comes from my early relationship with my father, and I'm working on that. Could you just help me with my feelings of rejection?'

"Conversely, Pat in the same situation might say it this way: 'I know you must be feeling rejected when I don't call. If I were waiting for you and you didn't call, I might feel the same way. Under the circumstances you have a right to your anger. When I think of your anger and the conflict between us, though, I feel anxious. I know this isn't coming from you. You just want my love. Can you help me with my uncomfortable feeling. so I can feel safer about being close?'"

Pat and Angie seem overwhelmed by all this. So I give them what I've just said on paper, so they can review it later.

"It's important that you practice these skills. After all, you are both committed to one another. When you ask for safety or acceptance, you're going to get a compassionate response from your partner. But more importantly, by accepting and taking responsibility, you create all kinds of space for the other person to voluntarily change their behavior. Their motivation for doing so is your pain. They don't want to be the source of your pain. As a result, it's far more likely that they will alter their approach. Using a defense that looks like an attack will never open the door to a voluntary change in behavior."

Chapter 16

Final Perspectives and Ending the Struggle

Pat's Perspective

Hi. It's hard to know where to begin. So much has happened. Let's see, Angie and I started therapy about nine months ago and stayed with it for about six months. I have to say, those were six of the most impactful and dramatic six months of my life.

When we started, I was absolutely convinced that I was right and Angie was wrong. I wanted to blame her. I wanted to get away from her. I knew that philosophically I wanted to get away from her anger. To me, anger was unacceptable and wrong, and the rest of the world was on my side in that point of view.

At the beginning, it seemed like Mark was missing the point. Didn't he know that I was right and she was wrong? He kept trying to change the subject. Then when he started talking about my father, I thought, "Here we go again, blaming the parents." I just didn't want to go over all of that again. I thought I had dealt with my Dad issues and forgiven him. Plus, it made me feel guilty even to think that my father had something to do with it. It was like telling a dirty little secret that I had promised never to tell.

Anyway, I began to see what Mark was doing. He was mapping out this very nuts-and-bolts model for how Angie and I were going about our relationship. He would diagram it over and over again on that big whiteboard of his. And despite the fact that I kept thinking that he was wrong, that the real issue was Angie's anger, there was a day when what he was doing suddenly dawned on me. He was laying down a map for me to see what *I* was doing.

At first, it was as if he thought he could read my mind. I would resist that with all my might. We Unicorns, I was to learn, don't like anyone reading us. But as time went on, I realized that he was trying to teach me something. Then I started to think. What in hell is he saying? It was only then that I had my first in a series of revelations. I didn't know what he had been saying because I wasn't listening. In fact, I wasn't even there. I would just shut down and go away.

The first time I noticed it was one night when he had one of his notorious diagrams on the board and was leading me through a series of questions. Suddenly I became aware of this feeling inside of me that kept saying, "What if I get the wrong answer?" Shit! There it was. Right there in the therapy session I was experiencing exactly what he was talking about on the board. He would ask me a question. I would think, "Oh no, what if I get the answer wrong?" Then I'd get real nervous and I could feel myself just go away inside. I was sitting in the chair in his office, but my mind was safe and protected hundreds of miles away feeling no feeling—no sensations at all. I noticed that my whole body would go numb when that nervous, anxious feeling started to come up.

It was then that I realized that Mark was giving me a map to follow what was going on inside of me. So I realized that I should start to use the map. But before I was able to do that, I remember asking over and over again, "So I'm nervous and anxious, what do I do?"

Mark kept telling me, "Do nothing. Just watch what you do." Of course, he was trying to teach me self-observation. He kept saying, "Just notice yourself doing what you do." I guess that night while he was talking to me, and I saw myself go away, was my first experience of truly watching myself. Gradually, I understood why I needed to watch myself. That's when I caught on to what he was saying.

What was weird was that as I learned to watch myself, I found myself avoiding, shutting down, and trying to escape all the time everywhere. It was like my thoughts were constantly being polluted by this overwhelming sense that I need to get away. To put it another way, it was as if every thought was a reaction supporting the need to escape.

I began to hear escape predicates in my language. There was this kind of "Yeah but what if I need to get away" theme behind the veil of my thoughts all of the time. Of course, along with this went the realization of how scared I was. Underneath the stream of thoughts was a constant hum of fear.

It was then that I was able to start questioning my experience—what Mark calls my perception. I vividly remember coming home one night and finding Angie waiting for me. She had this really distressed look on her face. Immediately I could hear my mind go, "Uh-oh!" My newfound awareness picked up on that reaction: I could feel myself bracing for an attack. Then I questioned myself: "Is there really going to be an attack coming?"

I asked Angie what was wrong. She told me that her sister had just called to tell her that her uncle had committed suicide. Angie had known that uncle since her childhood and had many fond memories of him. She was obviously shocked and hurt by the news. As I looked past my reaction to what I thought I saw in my wife's face, I could see how desperately she needed comforting. She needed me.

Great! There I had been trying to fight off this overwhelming need to run from an anticipated conflict. What a dope. The love of my life had just had a dagger stuck in her chest, and I was too uncomfortable to be available to her. Trust me, it wasn't a proud moment. It was then and there that I made a vow to try to constantly be aware of what is going on with me. It's something I practice. I'm not always good about it, and I do slip into my old habits. But now at least I'm able to see what I've done after the fact and own it.

Our relationship is better now than it has ever been. I've learned not to allow Angie's anger to push me away. I try to move toward her in some small way when I see it flare up. That effort always diffuses the emotion. It's not so bad anymore when it does come up. When I roll over in bed in the morning, I don't see this angry person like I used to. I see a little girl who just wants love and acknowledgment. I'm determined that she'll get that from me no matter what. I want to help her heal her heart. That has become more important than my need to run from the shadow of my father.

Angie's Perspective

You can tell that I'm conquering my Lion tendencies, since I let Pat go first. That was a little joke.

Let me see, where do I start? My perspective on life has undergone nothing short of an amazing transformation. I'm glad for the opportunity to talk about it from my personal perspective.

When Pat and I decided to get counseling, I was just like a ball of raw hamburger. Everything made me mad. I was unhappy all the time. I was desperately afraid that I would lose Pat. Every time he walked out the door, I knew I would have a battle on my hands just to get him to come home. Life couldn't have been more miserable. I had even started to develop physical symptoms from the stress. I was a wreck.

As you might expect, my mission in seeing Mark was to get Pat to change his ways. We needed a referee, I thought. Initially I was mad at Mark, because he clearly wasn't going to do what I wanted him to do. He kept talking about feelings. I knew how I felt—angry! What more was there? Then he started putting that crazy stuff on that whiteboard of his.

I guess I didn't mind so much having him talk about my pain. I could feel the pain, all right. But I had no way of expressing any of it without anger. What really got me was when he started talking about perception and all that brain stuff. I knew what I saw. I didn't need him telling me what perception is, for heaven's sake. I was right. I knew I was right. What was his problem? "Therapists," I thought, "they always think they're better than everyone else!"

I guess what turned me around about that was when I understood the circular relationship between my anger and Pat's avoidance. It truly was a flash of insight for me. Yet I felt helpless when I saw it. I mean, anger was all I knew. I didn't have any other tool in my kit to fix the problem. What was I supposed to do?

Then when Mark told me simply to watch myself being angry, I thought he had flipped his lid. Of course I could watch. I always knew when I was angry. I suppose it was when I started to realize that all of this somehow stemmed from my Dad that I started to listen more thoughtfully to what he was saying. At some point, things started to ring true and it occurred to me that he was seeing something in me that I wasn't seeing.

The idea of using self-observation—the mind minding the mind, I think he said—was new to me. One day I tried it and it was a really weird experience. I actually watched myself getting angry. I could feel the feeling coming up from somewhere deep inside my mind. Before I knew it, I felt the compulsion to act out, and I did. I saw myself start to yell. My Lord, I couldn't stop! It was then and there that I decided that this thing was not going to get the best of me. No matter what, I was going to get angry when *I* decided—not when *it* decided. Enough is enough!

Things started changing real fast. I went back to the model Mark kept putting on the board: Perception leads to feeling which leads to defensive behavior. I began working on feeling the feeling. This was hard because I thought the anger was the feeling. But there was a feeling there all right. What I discovered was that a split second before the anger came there was always that same old pain, a feeling like I wasn't "good enough," that kind of rejected feeling.

Practicing feeling the feeling was hard. I kept forgetting to do it; and then, the next day I would remember. But what I started to do was to think back, over the previous day or two, about times I remembered that I was angry. Then I would try to feel the hurt feeling that went with the anger. Sure enough, there it was—every time.

After a few days of doing that, I started getting pretty good at it. Then one day, Pat and I were arguing and, all of a sudden, I got a sense of the pain I was defending. There it was, just like that. I could feel that "not good enough" feeling.

A few days later, I was waiting for Pat to come home. He was late, of course. I started to get angry; I felt the rejection. Then I stopped myself and asked the next question, "What is my perception?" My perception was that what he was doing was personal; I was taking it personally. I realized that I take everything personally.

I questioned my perception. "Is it really personal?" Then I saw clearly for perhaps the fist time. It wasn't personal. Pat was probably out there stalling around, delaying coming home for fear of the inevitable conflict. When he got home, I wasn't angry. I threw my arms around him and told him how glad I was to see him and how much I love him. He looked at me as if I had blown a sprocket.

From that moment on, I just kept asking myself, "Is this personal?" The answer was no. I discovered that there is no worldwide conspiracy to make Angie's life miserable.

What happened next was a bit unexpected. I found that my awareness of my pain and of my distorting perceptions led to an ability to see through other people's behavior to their pain and perception. It was as if I could see everything that was going on!

Maybe that's what set up the next great revelation for me. One night at Mark's office, we had been talking about religion and the Bible and stuff. I can't remember exactly what I said, but Mark made a comment that stuck with me.

He said, "Let me tell you a secret, Angie. Your shame is an idol, a false god. Your brain literally recreates that pain every moment and your life is a response to that. As long as that process takes place without question, it impedes your awareness of the true divinity of each moment. So instead of basking in the full-time presence of God, you are committing idolatry. Whatever divine inheritance we can have in this life can't reach you because your mind is busy worshiping shame."

I thought about that a lot. Then I retraced my mental steps to see if it was true. I started looking for the pain of feeling not good enough. Sure enough, I found it everywhere in my thinking. It's a little hard to describe. It was as if shame was the default value by which I defined the rest of my life, the reference point for everything. If something good happened, I measured it against the shame. If something bad happened, I mentally compared it against the shame. In essence, everything in my mind was a value judgment made with respect to the backdrop of pain I felt.

I began literally to pray, every time I felt those negative feelings, "Show me what I'm supposed to see that I'm not seeing. What can I learn here? Open my eyes so I can see beyond the pain to what's actually here." This questioning and praying became an obsession for a while.

Then, one day, in a magic moment that I'll never forget, I saw a thread. In my mind, the thread connected my pain in the present to each and every moment I had ever felt it. I could see it extend back through my life into my childhood. Memories started coming up. I saw where my distortions and adaptive patterns had come from. It was my life laid bare.

As I saw clearly, for the first time, my programming and my emotional idolatry, I was reborn. Suddenly my pain and anger moved aside and I could see myself clearly for who I was before all the toxic waste got dumped into me. I experienced a sense of freedom and peace truly beyond description. I felt a oneness, a sureness in the universe. My insight released my soul. It was sobering as well as exhilarating. My life changed in that moment, forever. What I saw, what I experienced, could never be ripped from me by emotional reactivity. No matter how much darkness remained in me, I still knew the light that had been there all along.

Mark's Perspective

After looking back on the flow of information in this book and at the experiences of Pat and Angie, I find it useful to ask: "What is the purpose of my having written this book? On the surface, the answer seems obvious. The purpose is for you to find out if you're a Lion or a Unicorn, so you can understand the dynamics of your relationship and make it better. At least that must be one legitimate interpretation.

Let me make a rather bold assessment. I don't care if you're a Lion or a Unicorn. I don't care if my little theory is right. Maybe I have misunderstood brain functioning, and maybe I haven't. What if I really don't know anything about fear and shame? Sure, I've tried to build a logical sequence that makes sense to me for explaining people's behavior. But what if it's all wrong? What then? What then was or is the real purpose of the book?

The real purpose of the book is to give you a map that helps you look deeply inside of yourself. Developing awareness is the real purpose of this book. Taking you off automatic pilot is the real purpose. Entering into the freedom that comes from moving out of the prison of distorted perceptions, beliefs, and behaviors—that's the purpose.

Does that mean I think the Lion/Unicorn theory is wrong or built on a weak foundation? No, not at all. What it does mean is that it doesn't matter if you need to take exception to some aspect or another of my interpretation of relationships. If it helps you see how *you* operate inside, I've accomplished my goal.

Lions, Unicorns—who cares? Relationships are fulfilling when we really, really, really see who we are and really, really, really see who the other person is. To do that, we need to see into our own hearts. When we do, we paradoxically see into the heart of the other person. The compassion that comes from really seeing brings us close together, creating true intimacy.

Do Lions experience and defend against fear? Of course. Do Unicorns experience and defend against shame? Can we be a little of both? Yes. Are there Beavers and Elk, and Tigers as well? Possibly. Maybe Trout, too. This begs the real question, which is: Are there millions of sleepy, unconscious, profoundly unaware people in the world? Yes. And is that why relationships keep failing? *Absolutely!*

So, if you hear your mind screaming, "Yeah but, yeah but"—objecting to this part or that part of what I've presented here—then let the light of your awareness shine on the screaming. If you don't agree with me, notice that you don't agree. Check out what's happening inside of you. By what process do you end in disagreement? Learn the process, understand it, become the master of it. The key and my goal for you is self-inquiry. Without that everything is bondage.

What do we discover when we move beyond our misperceptions and distortions and the screaming in our heads? The direct experience of the world, of love, of beauty, of the oneness of the universe. And that includes, for those of us in relationship, the person we fell in love with and married, and who did the same with us.

THE END

Afterword: Lions vs. Unicorns

We're about halfway through the morning of the all-day Lion/Unicorn workshop. It's time for the panel exercise. We spent the first hour or so discussing the concept of temperament, and how it breaks down into the two types. One of my goals for the workshop is to get each person to look at his or her partner in a new and different way. My hope is that discovering that they are with a person who has a radically different worldview than their own will shift the energy in the relationship a little.

One of the ways I do this in the workshop is by setting up a panel. I divide the room into one group of Lions and one group of Unicorns.

"Now, here are the rules of the Lion/Unicorn panel. You can ask anyone on the opposite panel any question you like about what it's like to be a Lion or a Unicorn. But you can't ask your partner. This is very important, since we want you to see that your partner's experience is one that they share in common with many or all of the others of that type."

Don raises his hand. "Any question?"

"Any question, but it has to be related to the experience of being either a Lion or a Unicorn. What we're attempting to do is to understand the experience of the other type without getting into any conflict. So who wants to go first?"

There is predictable silence among the ten couples in the room. Pat and Angie are circulating among them, giving some encouraging nods here and there. They volunteered to assist my wife and me today. Finally, a hand goes up. Terry. predictably a Lion, asks the first question.

"What's it like being a Unicorn? I mean, do you experience the feeling that Mark was talking about earlier?"

149

The ten Unicorns exchange glances. Larry decides to speak up. "I'm not sure what you mean; but after listening to the descriptions this morning, I was able to identify something that I do. Mark was explaining that Unicorns avoid. I was able to identify a sort of going away or shutting down inside that I do. I have always done it, but it had never been pointed out to me so I never paid much attention to it."

Bertha chimes in: "I noticed that, too. But I've always done that. I just keep to myself for fear of what others might say or do. I always knew it was because of fear. It's interesting to hear Larry say he never noticed the feeling he was having."

I address Larry. "It sounds like you've had a pretty big insight today. What seems like a very small and natural thing to you may be a very large and significant thing in your relationship. I'm curious, Bertha, what do you think is the source of this 'keeping to yourself' thing that you do?"

"Oh, that's easy. I was raised in a family where my Dad was never around and my mother was the enforcer. She would yell at us and pull our hair. Sometimes she would slap us. I just learned to keep to myself, to shut down. Then she would never have a reason to come after me. I know I still do it today. It's almost like I can't help it."

Mary, one of the Lions, has a scowl on her face. "I just don't get all of this stuff about our parents. I love my parents. I don't want to go back and blame them. I'm angry. I know I'm angry. It's just the way I am. I don't want to get into all that stuff from the past."

Angie signals to me and I nod at her. She speaks up, "Mary, you have little girls, don't you?"

Mary replies that she does.

"Do you think your parenting and the example you set have an impact on them?"

"Of course."

"That's all we're saying. We all grew up in environments in which we learned certain ways of coping. We all learned to adapt to the family around us and to the parents we had. These patterns are what we're talking about."

Mary indicates that she understands and says, "But I don't want to go back to the past. I've dealt with all of that."

I decide to interject, "Mary, you're right. None of us wants to go back to the past. What we're trying to discover is how in fact we do unconsciously do that in the present anyway. When we have an emotional reaction,

150

we literally do go back to the past because that's where the reaction was learned. Going back to the family and finding someone to blame makes no sense at all—I agree with you. We're not interested in blaming mother or father for our problems. We're trying to discover the mother or father that lives in our heads. That's the source of the problem."

Janice raises her hand. "I want to know why you Lions take everything so personally."

"Because it is personal," says Jeffrey, "When someone ignores me or puts me down, that's personal. I'm not going to put up with that type of treatment."

Janice says, "You mean it feels like an attack to you? Can't you see that the other person is just insensitive?"

"I wish I could," Jeffrey says, shrugging his shoulders. "I'm seeing now that taking everything so personally is a kind of prison I live in. It fuels my anger. But yeah, to me, everything is personal."

Pat steps forward and says, "This was one of the hardest things for me to learn about Angie. So much of what happened to her she always took personally. When I started to study my reaction to her taking things personally, I noticed that I resisted seeing the situation from her perspective. Once I asked myself what it must be like to see everything as a personal attack, I suddenly knew what awful pain she must be in so much of the time. Then I came to grips with the fact that it didn't matter what my *judgment* was about her experience. What mattered was her experience, and in order to understand that fully, I had to get into her head and see it from her point of view."

"What's weird about what Pat just said," Angie interjects, "is that as soon as he started to see my point of view and validate it, I started to be less sensitive."

Another participant raises her hand. "Angie, let me ask you a question. From my Unicorn perspective, I'm beginning to see that you really needed Pat to come closer to you, to understand you, and to really listen to you. Is that right?"

"Yes." Angie looks at me and then turns back to the questioner. "For me, the hurt that I brought into the relationship, the thing that I wanted healed by Pat, was a large feeling that nobody cared about me. So I wanted him to *care*. I think that for Lions this has to come in the form of what you pointed out. I would call it a need for an emotional connection. For me, that signals that I'm cared for."

151

Jenny, one of the Lions, pipes up. "That reminds me of a question I would like to ask. What does it take to get you Unicorns to *connect*? It seems it's like pulling teeth!"

Douglas clears his throat and starts to talk. "I think I can answer that. I might be wrong in speaking for the rest of the Unicorns. But it's a feeling of wariness in the sense that my mind is telling me that what I say will be stupid or will be ridiculed. I remember when the teacher would call on me in school, I would get extremely anxious. What if I got the answer wrong? So I would do nothing but stammer until she ran out of patience and went on to someone else."

From across the room I see Doug's wife, Mary, as a look of shock comes over her face. "My God, Doug," she bursts out, "that's what's been going on? Oh my Lord! You mean you don't answer me because you're afraid to tell me the wrong thing?"

I decide to step in. "Just a moment, Mary. You might be onto something big here. But let's look a little deeper." I turn to Doug. "Doug, you seem to be in the middle of some epiphany right now. Am I right?"

"Yeah. I am realizing that the reason I dummy up so much is anxiety. I never saw that before."

I ask Doug, "When you think of giving someone the wrong answer, which parent comes to mind?"

I watch as he pauses and his eyes defocus, looking straight ahead. Finally, he looks up at me and says, "It's my Dad! If you gave him a wrong answer, you got the belt."

The conversation between the Lions and the Unicorns goes on for another twenty minutes or so. As it does, the questions become more and more earnest. It's becoming clear to me that the Lion and the Unicorns in the room are now aware that there is a basic biological and emotional difference between the two groups. This is a difference they have struggled to change in their partner but now must accept as reality. When the exercise is done, each will view their partner through a completely different lens than before.

Frequently Asked Questions

1. If two unicorns meet, do they repel each other? Or does one of them begin expressing latent leonine behavior? Or does one them project leonine behavior onto the other?

I don't know if they would repel each other. They just don't seem to be attracted to one another too often. That said, I do believe that two Unicorns, if they are near the center of the Lion/Unicorn continuum, may in fact get into a relationship. Then very often one assumes more of the predator role, and, yes, the process of projection takes place as well. However, the projection is not just one-way. Both parties will project disowned parts of themselves onto the other. The one who assumes the Lion role will project their weakness and vulnerability onto the Unicorn, while the Unicorn will project their anger onto the Lion.

2. Have you ever seen two Lions in a relationship?

No. Something tells me that it would just be too explosive. I can't imagine two Lions wanting to share the stage in a relationship with one another.

3. If someone resolves past trauma, is the person still triggered in the Lion/Unicorn circular fashion (Figure 3-4) Do their perceptions change?

No. I believe a person's perceptual frame around trauma may be radically different than the frame around their Lion/Unicorn patterns. Certainly, any therapy that results in healing and insight will dramatically aid a person's emotional maturity in a relationship. Often trauma is inextricably linked to the fear or shame that emerges in relationships, but I view these as separate therapeutic challenges.

4. What about guilt and jealousy?

Guilt is a feeling and jealousy is more of a behavior, like anger. I didn't include these distinctions in the book to keep things simple. Just as with any other feeling or behavior, the process starts with a perception. What perception drives guilt or jealousy and where does it come from? The answer comes through looking deeply and completely accepting the experience of the feeling. We need to see what the mind does as we watch the mind create the guilt or jealousy. By embracing it fully and accepting responsibility for it, we will see where it comes from.

5. Aren't you trying to blame parents?

Clients often tell me, "My parents did the best they could when they raised me." My comeback is usually, "What did they do? Did they read a book or take a parenting class?" Most parenting is a random process done by unconscious people. While blaming today for what happened yesterday makes no sense, assigning responsibility does make sense. Conditional love brings with it conditioning. Our conditioning is what keeps us trapped. Unfortunately, parents are responsible for that conditional love. By seeing this clearly, we take responsibility for the conditional love we are giving our children. Only then can the transgenerational cycle stop.

6. Can you switch Lion/Unicorn roles?

Not very often, but, yes, we all can be either predators or prey. I have seen relationships in which one person started as a Lion with the other as a Unicorn and then the relationship did a flip-flop. I've only seen this rarely, though.

7. What if I can't distinguish if I'm Unicorn or Lion? I share an equal part of both characteristics.

This question reveals something about the defenses of the person asking it. No one shares equal parts of any emotional aspect. This question tends to get asked by people who are only into the philosophy of the theory, who haven't really looked at themselves deeply or don't want to. In other words, the questioner usually is being defensive so as to not get the point.

8. How do I deal with my partner who doesn't see they are a Unicorn or Lion?

You were never meant to deal with your partner. Dealing with you is a big enough challenge. This question only comes when we resist clearly looking at ourselves and want our partner to change instead. Once we learn and grow to the fullest extent, the question answers itself.

9. Is it necessary to know who is the Unicorn or Lion in all my relationships?

No, just the most intimate and important ones. What's important isn't "labeling" but "knowing" —seeing clearly. Once you know what really happens in your mind, the distinction of Lion/Unicorn loses its importance. The Lion/ Unicorn model is a tool for awareness, not a panacea for unconsciousness.

Bibliography

Alford, B., & Beck, A. (1997). *The Integrative Power of Cognitive Therapy.* New York: The Guilford Press.

Allen, J. (2001). *Traumatic Relationships and Serious Mental Disorders.* New York: John Wiley & Sons.

Atkinson, B. (1999). The Emotional Imperative. *Family Therapy Networker,* 23(4), 22-31.

Bartholomew, K., & Shaver, P. (1998). *Methods of Assessing Adult Attachment: Do They Converge?* pp. 25-45). New York: The Guilford Press.

Belksy, J. & Rovine, M. (1987) Temperament and attachment security in the strange situation: An empirical rapprochement. *Child Development,* 58, 787-795.

Belksy, J., Rovine, M., & Taylor, D.G. (1984) The origins of individual differences in infant-mother attachment: maternal and infant contributions. *Child Development,* 55, 718-728

Booher, M. (2000). *Communication Within the Marital Dyad: An Attachment-Theoretical Perspective.* Austin, TX: The University of Texas at Austin.

Breunlin, D., Schwartz, R., & Kune-Karrer, B. (1992). *Metaframeworks, Transcending the Models of Family Therapy.* San Francisco: Jossey-Bass.

Carey, W. (1997). *Understanding Your Child's Temperament.* New York: Simon and Schuster.

Chess, S., & Thomas, A. (1984). *Origins & Evolution of Behavior Disorders: From Infacny to Adult Life.* New York: Brunner/Mazel.

Christensen, A. & Heavey, C.L. (1999). Interventions for Couples. *Annual Review of Psychology,* 50, 165-90.

Cramer, D. (2002). Linking conflict management behaviours and relational satisfaction: The intervening role of conflict outcome satisfaction. *Journal of Social & Personal Relationships* Vol. 19(3), 425-432

Crockenburg, S.B., (1981) Infant irritability, mother responsiveness, and social support influences on the security of infant-mother attachment. *Child Development* 52 (3):857-86.

Crohan, S. (1988). *The Relationship between Conflict Behavior and Marital Happiness: Conflict Beliefs as Moderators.* Ann Arbor, MI: The University of Michigan.

Crouch, J. (2002). *Divorce Statistics Collection.* Retrieved 7/19/02 from the World Wide Web: http://www.divorce reform.org/stats.html.

Davidson, R. (2004). What does the prefrontal cortex "do" in affect: perspectives on frontal EEG asymmetry research. *Biological Psychology* 67, 219-233.

Davidson, R. et al (2004). The privileged status of emotion in the brain. *Proceedings of the National Academy of Science.* 101 (33), 11915-11916.

Dawson, G., Klinger, LG., Panagiotides, H., Hill, D., & Spieker, S. (1992). Frontal lobe activity and affective behavior of infants of mothers with depressive symptoms. *Child Development,* 63(3), 725-37.

Dutton, D. (1995). *The Domestic Assault of Women* (Rev. ed.). Vancouver: UBC Press.

Dutton, D. (1998). *The Abusive Personality: Violence and control in intimate relationships.* New York: The Guilford Press.

Evans, J., & Abarbanel, A. (1999). *Introduction to Quantitative EEG and Neurofeedback.* San Diego: Academic Press.

Feeney, J. & Noller, P. (1990). Attachment Style as a Predictor of Adult Romantic Relationships. *Journal of Personality and Social Psychology,* 58(2), 281-291.

Finely, J. (2000). *The Contemplative Heart.* Notre Dame: Sorin Books.

Flowers, B. (2001). The limits of a technical concept of a good marriage: exploring the role of virtue in communication skills. *Journal of Marital and Family Therapy,* 27(3), 327-40.

Fox, NA. (1991). If it's not left, it's right. Electroencephalograph asymmetry and the development of emotion. *American Psychologist,* 46(8), 863-72.

Geffner, R. (2000). *Ending Spouse/Partner Abuse.* New York: Springer Publishing Company.

Goldsmith, H. and Davidson, R. (2004). Disambiguating the Components of Emotional Regulation. *Child Development* 75 (2), 361-365.

Gottlieb, M. (1999). *The Angry Self.* Phoenix, AZ: Zeig, Tucker & Co.

Henderson, H., Fox, N., & Rubin, K. (2001). Temperamental contributions to social behavior: the moderating roles of frontal EEG asymmetry and gender. *Journal of the American Academy of Child and Adolescent Psychiatry*, 40(1), 68-74.

Houston, T., Caughlin, J., Houts, R., Smith, S., & George, L. (2001). The Connubial Crucible - Newlywed Years as Predictors of Marital Delight, Distress, and Divorce. *Journal of Personality and Social Psychology*, 80(2), 237-252.

Irwin, W. et al. (2004), Amygdalar interhemispheric functional connectivity differs between the non-depressed and depressed human brain. *NeuroImage* 21, 684-686.

Kerr, M. & Bowen, M. (1988). *Family Evaluation.* New York: W. W. Norton & Company.

Kochanska, G. (1991) Patterns of inhibition to the unfamiliar in children of normal and affectively ill mothers. *Child Development* 62, 250-263.

Lewis, J. (1997). *Marriage as a Search for Healing.* New York: Brunner/ Mazel, Inc.

MacLean, A.P. (2001) *Attachment in Marriage: Predicting Marital Satisfaction from Partner Matching Using a Three-Group Typology of Adult Attachment Style.* West Lafayette, IN., Purdue University.

McMullin, R. (2000). *The New Handbook of Cognitive Therapy Techniques.* New York: W. W. Norton & Company.

McNulty, J. & Karney, B. (2002). Expectancy confirmation in appraisals of marital interactions. *Personality & Social Psychology Bulletin* 28(6), 764-775.

Middleberg, C. (2001). Projective Identification in Common Couple Dances. *Journal of Marital and Family Therapy*, 27(3), 341-52.

Mussen, P., Conger, J., Kagan, J., & Huston, A. (1990). Emotional and Social Development in Infancy. In P. Mussen, J. Conger, J. Kagan, & A. Huston (Eds.), *Child Development and Personality* (7th ed., pp. 135-178). New York: Harper Collins.

Nichols, M. and Schwartz, R. (1995). *Family Therapy Concepts and Methods* (3rd ed.). Boston: Allyn and Bacon.

Padesky, C., & Greenberger, D. (1995). *Mind over Mood.* New York: The Guilford Press.

Peter F. Newhouse (1998). *Investigating the Correlations Between Marital Temperament Types and Marital Satisfaction*. Santa Ana. California: Southern California University for Professional Studies.

Putnam, S., & Stifer, C. (2002). Approach and Inhibition in the First Year. *Developmental Science* 5(4), 441-451.

Rholes, W., Simpson, J., & Stevens, J. (1998). Attachment Orientation, Social Support, and Conflict Resolutions in Close Relationships. In J. Simpson, & W. Rholes (Eds.), *Attachment Theory and Close Relationships* (pp. 166-188). New York: The Guilford Press.

Rubin, Z. (1970). Measurement of romantic love. *Journal of Personality and Social Psychology*. 16, 265-273.

Scaer, R. (2001). *The Body Bears the Burden, Trauma, Dissociation, and Disease*. New York: The Hawthorne Medical Press.

Schore, A. (1994). *Affect Regulation and the Origin of the Self*. Hillsdale, NJ: Lawrence Erlbaum Associates.

Schwartz, R. (1995). *Internal Family Systems Therapy*. New York: The Guilford Press.

Simpson, J. & Rholes, W. (Eds.). (1998). *Attachment Theory and Close Relationships*. New York: The Guilford Press.

Sperry, L. (1999). *Cognitive Behavior Therapy of DSM-IV Personality Disorders*. Philadelphia, PA: Brunner/Mazel.

Stifer, C., & Braungart, J. (1995). The Regulation of Negative Reactivity in Infancy: Function and Development. *Developmental Psychology*, 31, 448-455.

Tidwell, M., Reis, H., & Shaver, P (1996). Attachment, attractiveness, and social interaction: A diary study. *Journal of Personality & Social Psychology*. 71(4), 729-745.

Trevarthen, C. (1996). Lateral asymmetries in infancy: implication for the development of the hemispheres. *Neuroscience and Biobehavioral Review*, 20(4), 571-86.

Watzlawick, P., Weakland, J., & Fisch, R. (1974). *Change: Principles of Problem Formation and Problem Resolution*. New York: W.W. Norton & Company.

Weeks, G., & L'Abate, L. (1982). *Paradoxical Psychotherapy: Theory and Practices with Individuals, Couples, and Families*. New York: Brunner/ Mazel.

West, M., & Sheldon-Keller, A. (1994). *Patterns of Relating: An Adult Attachment Perspective*. New York: The Guilford Press.

About Mark Waller

PROFESSIONAL PROFILE:

Mark Waller is an award winning author of four books and numerous articles. A licensed Marriage and Family Therapist, he has been a management consultant for over ten years and has conducted workshops for manufacturers, utilities, and the computer industry. He has lectured at the University of Wisconsin and George Washington University. Mark has a B.A. in Business, a Masters Degree in Counseling, and a Ph.D. in Psychology. He has extensive experience helping executives and couples, as well as groups.

Mark is a highly respected clinician and professional with a worldwide reputation for his interpersonal and communications skills. He is a demonstrated leader and innovator who is a professional platform speaker/trainer and has a proven track record of achievement in sales and marketing.

PERSONAL PROFILE:

Mark Waller had a midlife crisis and became a statistic. At 40, he was a successful technical consultant, and the author of three books on computers and electrical power. His first book was entitled *Computer Electrical Power Requirements*. His second book, *PC Power Protection*, was a Tab Book Club main selection. His third book, *Mark Waller's Harmonics*, established him as an acknowledged leader in the field of electrical power quality. He received The Award of Achievement from the Society of Technical Communications in the 1988–89 competition for an article written for *Byte Magazine*. At that time, he was named a "Finalist" in L. Ron Hubbard's "Writers of the Future" contest (he is not a Scientologist). He traveled the country giving workshops and consulting for companies such as Southern California Edison and The Jet Propulsion Laboratory. He taught classes at Georgetown University and the University of Wisconsin.

Then disaster struck. The economy, the marriage, and the lifestyle all collapsed at the same time. Mark had nothing left but pain and fear. During this dark night of the soul Mark experienced an *awakening*. This led to a career and life change. THE DANCE OF THE LION AND THE UNICORN, was born from new insight that followed.

Today Mark is a Licensed Marriage and Family Therapist in Southern California where he lives with his wife Teresa. His passion is helping others experience *awakening* as well.

Reader Survey

Please circle one answer.

Did you enjoy *THE DANCE OF THE LION & THE UNICORN*?   Yes   No
Please explain why or why not _____
_____
_____

Was it helpful?   Yes   No
Did you learn anything new?   Yes   No
Could you relate it to your own life or experience?   Yes   No
Did it make you want to take action?   Yes   No

What was your favorite part or concept? _____
_____
_____

Do you have any additional comments? _____
_____
_____

Would you be willing to write a review to be posted on Amazon.com? If so please go to their site and look up my book. Links for review submission are clearly posted. Thank you very much!

Can we add you to our e-mail newsletter list? Please print legibly.

_____

Would you like to be notified when Mark Waller comes to your area for a workshop or book signing? *Please make sure you give us your e-mail address.*

_____   Yes   No

Please fill out and mail to: Or scan and e-mail as an image file to:
Mark Waller   mail@markwaller.com
4195 Chino Hills Pkwy PMB 611   For more information go to
Chino Hills, Ca 917098   www.markwaller.com